BRADNER LIBRARY
SCHOOLCRAFT COLLEGE
18600 HAGGERTY ROAD
LIVONIA, MICHIGAN 48152

HD 53 .B76 1997

Brooking, Annie.

Intellectual capital

WITHDRAWN

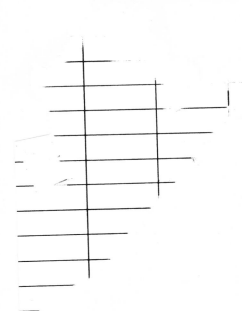

Intellectual Capital

This book is dedicated to mentors, to those who support and encourage others to succeed and in particular to Dr Hayes, Peter Marley, Dr John Beishon, Carolyn Morris, Antony Dick, my mother Margaret and my husband Andrew.

Intellectual Capital

Annie Brooking

INTERNATIONAL THOMSON BUSINESS PRESS

I(T)P An International Thomson Publishing Company

London • Bonn • Johannesburg • Madrid • Melbourne • Mexico City • New York • Paris
Singapore • Tokyo • Toronto • Albany, NY • Belmont, CA • Cincinnati, OH • Detroit, MI

HD
53
.B76
1997

Intellectual Capital

Copyright © International Thomson Business Press

I(T)P A division of International Thomson Publishing Inc.
       The ITP logo is a trademark under licence.

For more information, contact:

International Thomson Business Press
Berkshire House
168-173 High Holborn
London WC1V 7AA
UK

International Thomson Business Press
20 Park Plaza
Suite 1001
Boston, MA 02116
USA

Imprints of International Thomson Publishing

International Thomson Publishing GmbH
Königswinterer Straße 418
53227 Bonn
Germany

International Thomson Publishing Asia
221 Henderson Road #05–10
Henderson Building
Singapore 0315

Thomas Nelson Australia
102 Dodds Street
South Melbourne, 3205
Victoria
Australia

International Thomson Publishing Japan
Hirakawacho Kyowa Building, 3F
2-2-1 Hirakawacho
Chiyoda-ku, 102 Tokyo
Japan

Nelson Canada
1120 Birchmount Road
Scarborough, Ontario
Canada M1K 5G4

International Thomson Editores
Campos Eliseos 385, Piso 7
Col. Polenco
11560 Mexico D. F. Mexico

International Thomson Publishing South Africa
PO Box 2459
Halfway House
1685 South Africa

International Thomson Publishing France
1, rue St. Georges
75 009 Paris
France

All rights reserved. No part of this work which is copyright may be reproduced or used in any form or by any means – graphic, electronic, or mechanical, including photocopying, recording, taping or information storage and retrieval systems – without the written permission of the Publisher, except in accordance with the provisions of the Copyright Designs and Patents Act 1988.

Products and services that are referred to in this book may be either trademarks and/or registered trademarks of their respective owners. The Publisher/s and Author/s make no claim to these trademarks.

Whilst the Publisher has taken all reasonable care in the preparation of this book the Publisher makes no representation, express or implied, with regard to the accuracy of the information contained in this book and cannot accept any legal responsibility or liability for any errors or omissions from the book or the consequences thereof.

British Library Cataloguing-in-Publication Data
A catalogue record for this book is available from the British Library

Library of Congress Cataloging-in-Publication Data
A catalog record for this book is available from the Library of Congress

First Printed 1996

ISBN 1-86152-023-9

Cover Designed by Button Eventures
Typeset by Lorraine Hodghton
Printed in the UK by Clays Ltd, St Ives plc

http://www.thomson.com/itbp.html

CONTENTS

LIST OF FIGURES

LIST OF TABLES

ACKNOWLEDGEMENTS

I would like to thank those who helped me to research and write this book. Firstly, those whose early support helped to get the book started – Gordon Ewan of ICL, Dr Alan Smith of Laporte, Brian Sear of VenRad, Carolyn Morris of MAXWEST, Dr Paul Quintas of the Open Business School, Dave Hatter of Chapman and Hall and Brian Oakley. Many supported the research and preparation of the manuscript, in particular James Manning, Ben Rayner, Enrico Motta, Alex Goodall, David Wilson, Rob van der Speck, Min Basadur and Karl Wiig. I had wonderful support from all my colleagues at The Technology Broker, in particular from Nicky Sutton, Edward Taylor, Maureen Firlej, Caroline York, Peter Wharton, Bill Blake, Tori Walsh, Peter Board and Louise Lane.

I'd like to thank Ingmar Folkmans, my commissioning editor at International Thomson Publishing, who nursed me through this, my first book. He kept his cool when I missed my deadlines and looked serene when I said I wanted the colour of the title on the cover to match my nail polish and my favourite wedding hat.

Finally thanks to my husband Andrew – I can help to plant the seed potatoes now!

1

The Third Millennium Enterprise

Since the advent of computers and information technology, the nature of the enterprise has changed. We rely on different methods and skills than those of our predecessors in order to access our customers and provide them with goods and services. These new skills have been developed as a result of information technology, telecommunications technology and the requirement for a more sophisticated work-force which relies on expertise and technology more than manual labour.

THE IMPACT OF INFORMATION TECHNOLOGY

Information technology has not just replaced manual methods of working, but has enabled the creation of new services which were not previously possible. Examples include international banking services supported by modern telecommunications, credit card transactions of all types and even the booking of airline travel. Employees have changed the way in which they work. Some don't even have a 'place of work' any more, but instead work from their homes, communicating with their managers and colleagues via the information highway. These 'teleworkers' enable the enterprise to operate at greatly reduced cost, with fewer offices, fewer meeting rooms, reduced travel and savings in time and money.

To provide such services we have produced employees with new skills. Organizations depend on people who use computers as part of their day-to-day job. Their know-how is frequently a long time in the making. They use technology to communicate with customers and deliver products and services. Databases tell us what products and services to sell to a particular customer and record his buying history, product preferences and so on. Computers are used to monitor our credit card spending and recognize changes in our buying habits. This technology has been developed in order to help credit card companies identify fraudulent use of credit cards and catch the thief in the act.

Market Space not Market-Place

A new place to sell goods and services has emerged – the 'market space', a virtual market-place which lives on the Internet. Using the World Wide Web, companies can offer goods and services for sale and accept payment. The Web provides a virtual shop-front whilst the physical goods are delivered in the real world. Companies whose products can be digitized such as music, video games and computer software can complete the entire transaction in the market space, delivering goods in digital form via the Internet to the customer's computer.

Local has Become More Global

The global economy means that enterprises have global markets. In a multicultural market, symbols must be created so that the customer can associate with the enterprise no matter which country he lives in or what language he speaks. Trade marks such as the Mercedes star are more valuable to the enterprise than its factories. The mark is the prize, the factory merely the mechanism for delivering the vehicle which bears it. The value of smokestacks to the enterprise is diminishing relative to the value of intangible assets.

Merchandising Intangibles

Considerable sums of money change hands when film and cartoon characters are merchandised. In 1974, a Disney Productions Annual Report indicated royalty revenues of over $15,000,000 while in 1978 the Disney Merchandising Division sold $27,000,000 in merchandise. In 1978, the film Star Wars was quoted at one point as having generated $25,000,000 from box office receipts and $22,000,000 from licensed goods. Cy Schneider in *Advertising Age,* stated that Kenner Products sold over $100,000,000 worth of Star Wars merchandise. He also points out that Mary Poppins by Walt Disney was a 'saleswoman' for 46 manufacturers and sold everything from umbrellas to luggage to shoe polish. His estimate of the retail value of licensed goods and services from cartoon characters in 1978 was $2.1 billion and for 1979 $3.1 billion. Such revenues can be considered as concept revenue, which can only be realized in a global economy where the image of Mickey Mouse and his pals transcend all cultures and languages and are positioned in the market place as appealing to the consumer.

To Patent or Not to Patent?

Companies live or die by their competitive advantage. Or lack of it. Many organizations undertake research and development as a means of developing new technology which they believe will give them a competitive advantage. One of the ways in which technological innovation is protected is via a patent. Indeed, league tables are prepared which show who is filing the most patents and many speeches have been made condemning the lack of filings of Europe and the USA compared with Japan. But do these statistics really mean anything? Is the final goal of R&D to file a patent? Or is it to develop know-how through the process of performing the R&D? True, a patent gives the inventor a monopoly for a number of years. But in order to gain the monopoly the invention has to be disclosed. So it's not a secret any more, the competition knows how it works.

League Table of Patent Filings for 1993

Germany	48,774
France	16,040
UK	34,166
Japan	380,035
Korea	47,344
USA	191,386

Patents are very valuable protection for inventors. They are a 'Keep Off' sign for others who would violate the monopoly the patent grants the inventor. But should another ignore the 'Keep Off' sign it's necessary to take legal action, either to make them stop infringing or make them pay for the privilege of using the patent. If the patent is not enforced its value is questionable. If violators are not taken to court they will continue to infringe. This is bad news for the inventor who can't afford legal action and many would say that a patent is only worth what the organization is prepared to spend in enforcing it.

Some patents have a short life. The market window for many technologies can be very slim. Many patents are filed which don't have the potential to generate revenue for the inventors. One patent describes a mousetrap for the discerning mouse with a choice of cheese!

So what's the value of a patent? And why do organizations spend thousands of dollars filing them each year? Do organizations which file lots of patents have great competitive edge? Sometimes. For example, the Taq patent. Taq polymerase is the thermostable enzyme which allows amplification of a specific genetic sequence in genetic fingerprinting, also known as the polymerase chain reaction. The rights to both the enzyme and the polymerase chain reaction were owned by the Cetus corporation. In 1991 they sold the rights to Roche for $300 million. The pharmaceutical industry is littered with such examples but other industries do not follow its example. The European Commission in Brussels has stated that 30% of all R&D undertaken in Europe is duplicated. So why don't companies evaluate build-or-buy options and license technology rather than rediscover it? There are three possible reasons. Firstly, they don't know the work has been done. Secondly, the organization suffers from NIH (not

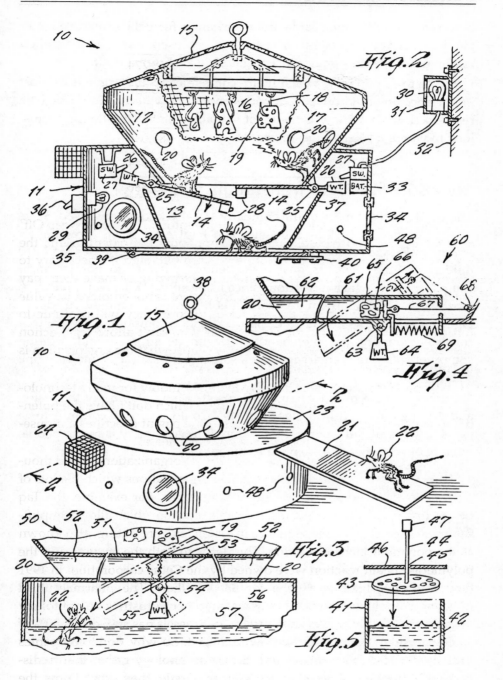

Figure 1.1 Mousetrap for the discerning mouse

invented here); in other words, the engineers believe they can do a better job than their predecessors. Or lastly, it is because know-how developed in pursuit of the final goal is just as valuable as the goal itself.

The last reason is one which many companies would argue is of most importance. In our knowledge based economy the value of R&D has to be reassessed. If know-how is the most valuable commodity then we must look to where it's kept – inside people.

Microsoft – A Third Millennium Company?

Microsoft is a third millennium company. It's also know-how based. Since it was founded in 1975 by Bill Gates and Paul Allen it has grown at an amazing average rate of 31% per annum, with reported revenues of $7,210 million in June 1995. Its goal is to deliver software to non-technical computer users, which it has done since its inception. Microsoft is also the most valuable company in the world. Yet Microsoft's competitive advantage comes from its ability to design and create computer software to a consistent quality and merchandise it with its strong brand. Writing computer software is an art and Microsoft is able to attract some very fine staff.

But what is the brand value of Microsoft? Many would say the vision and driving force of its founder Bill Gates. Could Microsoft continue to be as great without Bill Gates? If the value of the company is in the people what happens when they leave the company?

THE VALUE OF LEADERS

In a 1995 article the UK newspaper, *The Sunday Times*, reported on the value of some of the leaders of high profile companies, their remuneration and their impact on the company should they leave for one reason or another. Its findings show that for some key individuals the old adage 'no one is irreplaceable' is no longer true.

Of course the value of know-how is not just related to high profile individuals like Richard Branson and Bill Gates. Every organization has its key individuals whose absence would have a negative impact on the organization. The amount of money an organization spends in reinventing

Bill Gates	Chairman Microsoft Revenues $5bn a year
Value to company:	Rates as its 'five star general' and has a personal $7bn stake in the company to prove it. Gates is perceived as the world's most important company director.
Comment:	Losing Bill Gates would not just cost Microsoft, it could change the face of the communications revolution.
Martin Sorrell	Chief Executive WWP Group Market Capitalization £875m
Value to company:	Precisely rated at £28m over five years if he lifts the share price above 304p and hits his performance targets. Bonus package approved by about 75% of shareholders.
Comment:	Undermines the 'anyone can run an ad agency' jibe which cost Maurice Saatchi his job.
Anita Roddick	Chief Executive of the Body Shop Market capitalization £250m
Value to company:	Paid a modest £142,000 last year but Roddick's unusually strong association with the chain of stores adds value – possibly up to £12m – to the shares.
Comment:	Unique presence in brand equity for a retailer. Departure could shake the company.
Richard Branson	Chairman Virgin Group
Value to company:	From piloting airlines to launching colas and radio stations, every Virgin product has Branson's personal input. The value of the PR Branson personally generates is 'tens of millions of pounds'.
Comment:	Without Branson there is no Virgin for most analysts. The effect on the value of the company for most analysts is hard to assess.

Table 1.1 The value of leaders

expertise is considerable and ranges from figuring how to do something trivial like raising a purchase order, to mammoth tasks such as getting rid of industrial waste.

Lost expertise is a huge problem few companies have attempted to solve. Early attempts at building expert systems – computer systems which could emulate the behaviour and even analytical technique of an expert in a field such as fault diagnosis – have had limited success. This is largely due to the mismanagement of expectation by early expert systems developers, but the concept has been proven and is valid. It is clear that computer systems have a role to play in keeping track of corporate knowledge via a 'corporate memory' and corporate memory will become a key asset for the third millennium enterprise.

Employees are paid for a working day of seven or eight hours. A recent survey undertaken by the Gottilieb Duttweiler Foundation, the Swiss think-tank which has undertaken studies into knowledge management, has found that only about 20% of knowledge which is available to the company is actually used. This indicates that there is room for greater efficiency, profits, growth, competitive edge and so on, by just managing the knowledge within the organization more efficiently. Knowledge is an asset and like all assets has to be managed. Imagine what would happen to the state of the organization if all physical assets like factories, offices, machines were utilized only 20% of the time.

WHY THE LEARNING ORGANIZATION?

Training is one way in which the value of an individual to the organization is developed and maintained. Corporate training is subject to various fashion trends. Two current favourites are the Learning Company and Life Long Learning.

The former is a concept where the organization sees itself as a mechanism for nurturing employees, the latter where the organization sees itself as the customer of the individual employee and his expertise – the onus being on the individual to maintain himself as a desirable asset. Both approaches have their merits, but only if used in conjunction with an understanding of the company's strategic goals. If people are considered as a corporate asset, then training is their maintenance. Maintenance programmes which deliver efficiency are also assets, so therefore corporate training is one of the major ways in which employees of the third millennium enterprise will receive nourishment.

Corporate Memory Loss

Every time we lose an employee we lose a chunk of corporate memory. Despite the fact that the organization pays for people – their assets – by way of salary and invests in them by way of training, fast track plans and so on, the asset (the employee) is not owned by the organization, which is powerless to prevent its employees pursuing life-threatening hobbies every weekend such as bungee jumping or pot-holing.

How Barings Bank Went Bust

If people are an asset then effective people management is an asset too. Barings Bank is an example of an old company which failed due to lack of an appropriate management infrastructure.

Their star trader in the Singapore office, Nick Leeson, was given responsibility for both trading on the floor of the stock exchange and resolving the position in the back office. This responsibility, which he allegedly abused, gave him the opportunity to misrepresent the company's position to his peers and superiors. The scam was perfected by staffing the back office with junior staff members who had neither the experience nor the seniority to identify any inconsistencies in the books and raise the alarm with Leeson's bosses.

The absence of management control enabled £742 million, twice the value of the fixed assets of the bank, to be sent out to Singapore to fund Leeson's derivatives speculation. This was compounded by a questionable management decision to have the same person, Leeson, in charge of both the front and back offices. Coinciding with these failings was an individual who allegedly took advantage of the situation and single-handedly generated losses for Barings Bank of £827 million. Barings Bank, which had sprung from a trading company founded in 1762, with total assets of £5.9 billion in 1993, was sold on March 6 1995 to the Dutch financial giant ING for £1.

THE IMPACT OF CORPORATE CULTURE

This situation was allowed to develop at Barings largely as a result of the corporate culture at Barings Securities – the business for which Leeson worked. Securities was a young person's company. They worked and played hard. They earned huge bonuses for success in a macho culture which encouraged young people to 'go for it'. This culture, perceived as an asset, became a liability. It was also incompatible with the long established, low risk culture of Baring Brothers Bank. The management gap, which Leeson allegedly used to his advantage, broadened following the decision to bring the two very different Barings businesses together.

Corporate culture can be a very valuable corporate asset. The invisible bonds which hold the organization together are change resistant. This is an asset when the culture is beneficial to a healthy organization, but not when the culture represents some form of danger to the organization as a whole.

Research undertaken by The Technology Broker indicates that the single largest reason (80%) for the failure of collaborations is incompatible corporate cultures. It has become normal business practice for companies to collaborate on distribution, research, training and many other aspects of business. Having a culture which means you are 'easy to work with' is therefore a business asset, the limitations of which need to be well understood and the benefits maximized.

THE PROFILE OF THE THIRD MILLENNIUM COMPANY

So what will the third millennium enterprise look like? Its work-force is valuable because of what it knows. Good training is an asset, as it maintains the work-force and its know-how. Employees don't have as many face-to-face meetings as before, communicating electronically instead. They don't have to come to a place of work every day as they communicate with colleagues and managers via computers and networks. Many are teleworkers, working from home. The trade marks which represent the enterprise and its identity can have more value than its factories. Business is conducted in market space on the Internet and customers are serviced, tracked and marketed to via a myriad of technology. Remove the computer systems, the e-mail and the knowledge of how to use computer systems and the enterprise can't function. Lose the employee knowledge and it takes years to reinvent it. Lose the trademark and the businesses has no value. It's clear that in many enterprises the value is not in the tangible assets but in the intangible ones.

Do Accounts Reveal the True Value of the Enterprise?

No. Management and accounting methods are currently not set up to value and grow these assets. Investors in companies have to be super sleuths in order to locate hidden value within the enterprise. It is arguable that companies lacking intangible assets have no long-term value at all. We are hiring and firing without considering the long-term impact on the organization. Organizations still treat training as a staff privilege and pat themselves on the back for an average of five days per annum for each employee. We still view the company via the double-entry accounting method, invented five hundred years ago, which is based on tangible assets and does not reflect the true value of the third millennium enterprise.

Intangible and Ignored

In a recent survey of 226 FT 500 companies (the UK equivalent of the Fortune 500), 76% had not assigned any value to intangible assets in their annual report. Where intangible assets were included on the balance sheet, it mostly referred to goodwill generated by mergers and acquisitions. Goodwill is treated as a catch-all for a variety of monies which don't quite fit anywhere else. Directors of companies have a duty to ensure that the assets of companies in their charge are protected and exploited to the benefit of the enterprise and its shareholders. Such guidelines are set out in documents on corporate governance. Whilst the continuing management of cash, buildings and machinery is essential to the success of third millennium enterprises, that must be balanced by effective management of intangible assets to gain competitive advantage. Today, most enterprises do not know what their intangible assets are, what they are worth or how to manage them. All that must change.

2

The Emergence of Intellectual Capital

Intellectual capital is not new. It's been around since the first vendor established a good relationship with a customer. Then it was called goodwill. What has happened over the last two decades is an explosion in key technical areas including information technology, the media and communications, giving us new tools with which we have built a global economy. Many of these tools bring intangible benefits, which never existed before and which now we take for granted. The organization can no longer function without them, their ownership provides competitive advantage. Therefore they are an asset.

Intellectual capital is the term given to the combined intangible assets which enable the company to function.

IC Concept#1

Enterprise = Tangible Assets + Intellectual Capital

THE COMPONENTS OF INTELLECTUAL CAPITAL

The intellectual capital of an enterprise can be split into four categories:

- Market assets
- Intellectual property assets
- Human-centred assets
- Infrastructure assets

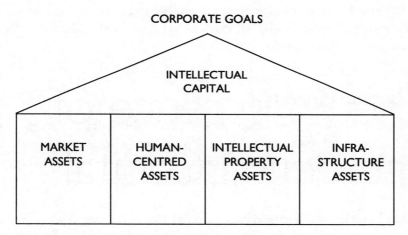

Figure 2.1 The components of intellectual capital

Market Assets

Market assets are the potential an organization has due to market-related intangibles. Examples include various brands, customers and their loyalty, repeat business, backlog, distribution channels, various contracts and agreements such as licensing, franchises and so on.

Why are Market Assets Important?

Market assets are important because they give a company a competitive advantage in the market-place. Branding denotes ownership and identity of products and services; customer loyalty ensures repeat sales leading to a healthy backlog. A good distribution channel ensures the entire market of potential customers can be serviced and that revenues from product and service sales is maximized. Favourable contracts ensure less expensive or guaranteed service, such as advertising or product sales, giving a company an advantage over competitors who may not enjoy similar privileges.

Market assets ensure that customers know the identity of the company and what it does. From time to time a company mismanages its marketing strategy and generates confusion in the market-place. When customers are confused they don't buy. Effective positioning strategies ensure that when a customer hears a company name the thought that enters the mind of the customer is the thought the company would wish him to have. Huge sums of money are put behind promotional campaigns which reinforce positioning strategies. 'At Avis we try harder', 'Beans Means Heinz', 'Intel Inside' and so on.

Intellectual Property Assets

Intellectual property (IP) assets include know-how, trade secrets, copyright, patent and various design rights. They also include trade and service marks. Some companies register thousands of patents every year, a large number of which are not exploited in the market.

Why is Intellectual Property Important ?

Intellectual property represents the legal mechanism for protecting many corporate assets. New devices leading to products or their component parts can be protected by one or more patents. Patents are valuable as they give the owner a monopoly on the patented invention for a period of time which is typically from 17–20 years; it varies from country to country. Patents are of particular value when they are embedded in products as it protects them from others who may want to copy the invention. Copyright protects the written word and is typically used to protect books, music and computer software. Market assets such as brands are protected by trade and service marks. Finally, trade secrets are protected by non-disclosure agreements, which means that the party who becomes privy to the secret agrees not to tell anyone other than those identified in the non-disclosure agreement. That said, the best way to keep a trade secret is not to tell anybody. The highest profile trade secret is probably the Coca-Cola formula, which is reputed to be shared between two individuals, each knowing half the formula!

Human-centred Assets

Human-centred assets comprise the collective expertise, creative and problem solving capability, leadership, entrepreneurial and managerial skills embodied by the employees of the organization. They also include psychometric data and indicators on how individuals may perform in given situations, such as in a team or under stress. We promote a viewpoint that we are not only looking at an individual in order to perform a particular job function, but view the individual as a dynamic entity who may fit into a variety of jobs over time. It is the job of a good manager to ensure that each human 'asset' has access and opportunity to mechanisms which enable the employee to achieve their full potential within the organization.

Why are Human-centred Assets Important?

Human-centred assets are the qualities which make up people. It may seem silly to ask why people are important but it's worth thinking about for a while. There are no businesses which can operate without at least one person. However, unlike market, intellectual and infrastructure assets, human-centred assets cannot be owned by the company. This should mean that they receive special treatment, but sadly they often don't.

Humans are expensive to hire, train and sustain. They also have the right to leave their employment, get sick, go on holiday and in general damage themselves via a wide range of hobbies and pastimes. As they become proficient and then excel in their employment, they learn more and become more valuable. But the knowledge in the head of the individual belongs to the person – not the company. So it's important to understand the skills, knowledge and expertise of the individual in order to know how and why someone is valuable and what role they should play within the organization. The optimal position for the organization to be in is to be able to derive maximum benefit from an individual being in employment with the company. That should be balanced by way of compensation – monetary, professional, personal development and opportunity. To do this properly is time consuming. Don't just consider the cost – but whether or not the third millennium enterprise can afford **not** to do it.

Infrastructure Assets

Infrastructure assets are those technologies, methodologies and processes which enable the organization to function. Examples include corporate culture, methodologies for assessing risk, methods of managing a sales force, financial structure, databases of information on the market or customers, communication systems such as e-mail and teleconferencing systems. Basically, the elements which make up the way the organization works. But we are not talking about the value of the tangibles which comprise the computer system and so on, but the way in which it is used in the organization. A good example is the Internet. Use of the Internet is free. It also doesn't belong to anyone, so it won't appear on anyone's balance sheet. However, the ability to use the Internet to sell goods means it is providing the organization with a distribution channel, therefore it is an asset. Such assets are peculiar to each business and their value to the organization can only be attained by survey. Sadly, the acquisition of infrastructure assets is frequently the result of some crisis, positioning them as a necessary evil rather than the structure which makes the organization strong and efficient.

Why are Infrastructure Assets Important?

Infrastructure assets are important because they bring order, safety, correctness and quality to the organization. They also provide a context for the employees of the organization to work and communicate with each other.

Marketing the value of infrastructure assets to the individual within the organization is important, in order to ensure they understand what they are supposed to do in given situations and how they contribute to the achievement of corporate goals. However, infrastructure assets should not be perceived as law and must change and bend to reflect changes in the market and workplace. Organizations which do not regularly question the value and effectiveness of infrastructure assets lose the edge which makes them win in the market-place.

WHY IS INTELLECTUAL CAPITAL IMPORTANT?

One hundred years ago labour was cheap. The value of the enterprise was measured in terms of smokestacks, machinery and cash. In the third millennium labour will not be cheap. The human-centred assets a company needs to operate will be rare and expensive commodities. It will take years of investment to create valuable market, infrastructure and intellectual property assets. Many companies, especially service oriented businesses, don't need many tangible assets to exist. Computers, communications and knowledge provide corporate bedrock for third millennium companies.

The market is homogenizing. No single organization brought about the change. It resulted from the widespread use of communications, information technology and the use of the media. The market has expanded for most growing businesses and at the same time has become more accessible. A trade mark which was only meaningful in a local community at the beginning of the century can now be known all over the globe.

Twenty years ago we weren't bothered with intellectual capital. Its emerging importance reflects the organization's increasing dependence on intangible assets. New types of companies are born every day which have only intangible assets. Their products are intangible and can be distributed electronically in the 'market space' via Internet. Such media and knowledge intensive companies whose products are digital are third millennium enterprises. The world has changed again and we must find new ways of monitoring and managing the organization which reflect that change.

The Intellectual Capital Indicator

Answer true or false to the following statements:

1 In my company every employee knows what his job is and how it contributes to corporate goals.
2 In my company each employee is treated as a rare asset, and management strive to fit each person into the optimal job.
3 Every employee in my company has the opportunity to create a career plan with the company.
4 In my company we evaluate ROI on R&D.
5 In my company we identify know-how generated by R&D.
6 In my company we know who our repeat customers are.
7 In my company we evaluate ROI on the distribution channel.
8 In my company we have a proactive intellectual property strategy.

9   In my company we audit all our licensing deals.

10 In my company we ensure there is synergy between employee learning programmes and corporate goals.

11 In my company the position we have in the mind of the prospect is the same as we promote.

12 In my company we know the value of our brands.

13 In my company every scientist and engineer understands the rudiments of patent protection.

14 In my company we generate new intellectual capital through business collaboration.

15 In my company our management processes make us strong.

16 In my company there is the infrastructure to help the employees do a good job.

17 In my company there is a mechanism to capture employees' recommendations to improve any aspect of the business.

18 In my company employees are quickly rewarded for helping the company to achieve its corporate goals.

19 In my company we understand the innovation process and encourage all employees to participate within it.

20 In my company our corporate culture is one of our greatest strengths.

The more 'no' answers the more you need to focus on strengthening your company's intellectual capital.

IC Concept#2

Intellectual Capital Sharpens the Cutting Edge

3
Market Assets

Market assets are those which are derived from a company's beneficial relationship with its market and customers. They comprise the brands, reputation, repeat business, distribution channels, favourable licensing and other types of contracts which give a company competitive advantage. Market assets are often the reason a company is acquired for a sum far greater than its book value. This occurs when others perceive that a company has market assets which are not being maximally exploited and that with a different strategy or management team they would generate increased wealth from under-exploited assets.

The Nestlé Acquisition of Rowntree

In their report for The David Hume Institute on the Nestlé takeover of Rowntree, Evan Davis and Graham Bannock analyse the reasons why Nestlé chose to pay more than double the quoted share price in its acquisition of Rowntree. On June 23rd the Nestlé acquisition of Rowntree was announced for £2.55 billion, ($US 3.8 billion). Nestlé wanted to move into the growing area of countline products – products sold by the piece – and

Rowntree had a stable of very successful brands including Kit-Kat, Aero, Polo, Yorkie, After Eight and Smarties. One of the appealing factors for Nestlé was the longevity of the brands owned by Rowntree. Successful chocolate confectionery brands are also virtually inflation proof and can be used as bargaining power to ensure distribution of other house brands through sales outlets. For Nestlé, the most strategic motive for joining the battle for Rowntree was to expand its interests in confectionery, particularly in the growing countline sector of the market. As early as 1987, Nestlé had identified an alliance with Rowntree as an objective, as it was the only route which would enable Nestlé to achieve its strategic goals other than organic growth – building up its own count lines – a long, high risk and costly process.

At the same time Rowntree was also trying to expand into other EC countries and the US. There was great synergy between Rowntree's need for an extended distribution channel and Nestlé's need for countline products. When Nestlé bought Rowntree it acquired several valuable market assets – the Rowntree brands, its market share and position and their customer loyalty.

THE POWER OF BRANDS

The brand is probably the most obvious market asset that most of us are aware of. Examples include Coca-Cola, Marlboro, IBM, Rowntree, Yamaha, Ferrari and so on. The rapid growth of communications and computer technology has had a homogenizing effect on world markets enabling corporations to undertake global branding strategies. Such strategies give companies the option of customizing products and services for local markets.

Brands are powerful reminders to customers to buy the products and services of one company in preference to another. Consider two brands A and B, where A is 10% more expensive than B. The content of the product may be identical, even coming from the same production line. Brand A is dominant and has greater market share and customer loyalty. The increase in revenue to the company selling Brand A can be attributed to the added value of the brand. The brand is an intangible asset.

There are several types of brand, all of which are market assets.

Product Brands

A product brand is used to distinguish one brand from another – Nescafé from Maxwell House, Lotus 123 from Excel, Ariel from Persil, Martini from Cinzano. How companies position and manipulate brands from each other can be very different. Some, such as laundry detergents, focus on the content of the product – with or without bleach, bio or non bio. Others, such as Martini, on positioning the product via the particular social sets who drink it.

Service Brands

Service brands typically tell us about a service. Rarely do they tell us about how the service itself is undertaken, but about its quality, reliability and so on. Examples of service brands include American Express, Hertz, and Federal Express. Now renamed FEDEX, Federal Express always had a reputation of reliability, efficiency and friendliness. When a package required a courier service people would say, 'Let's fedex it', even though they used an alternative courier service. It will be interesting to see how their revenues fare having committed genericide – we predict for the better. Also will American Express follow suit and rename itself the Amex?

Corporate Brands

Corporate brands are those where the company name has a presence, meaning and therefore value in the market-place. Examples include General Motors, IBM and Nestlé. The products of these companies are typically grouped so that there is some notion of 'core business' – cars, computer products and services and food products. Virgin is an exception. The Virgin group of companies is diverse: its interests include hotels, airlines, cola, vodka, radio post-production, retail stores and video games, to name a few. Each uses the Virgin brand name. This is unusual, as what are being positioned in the market are the attributes of the brand. NOP, a polling organization, conducted a survey for *PR Week*, (a UK trade publication) which confirmed that 80% of respondents linked the Virgin name with friendliness and a similar amount with high quality. Between 60% and 70% of respondents felt Virgin symbolizes innovation, fun and low prices. Virgin boss Richard Branson, a high profile figure, is the darling of the British. A very successful, self-made entrepreneur, he is also known for his dare-devil ballooning and speed boat expeditions. People buy a Virgin product because it is owned by Richard Branson who, according to a MORI survey of British young people for the BBC, was rated alongside Mother Theresa as being the person they would most trust to revise the Ten Commandments.

How are Brands Nourished and Sustained?

Unless exercised and nourished, brands lose value. The primary nourishment for brands is advertising and other forms of promotion. So in a tough market situation such as a recession, cutbacks in advertising and promotion can devalue brands. It's like failing to maintain a tangible asset such as a vehicle or building – after a time they lose value. It takes a great deal of time to build a brand of value and it must be nourished and protected all the time. The legal mechanism of protecting a brand is via a trade or service mark which we talk more about later.

┌─ IC Concept#3 ────────────────────────────────┐
│   │
│   Brands Outlive Companies   │
│   │
└──┘

Why Value Brands?

Assigning value to brand assets helps to prioritize when resources to nourish and protect them are scarce. The most obvious time to value a brand is when considering selling the company or its brands. But unless your brand is akin to Coca-Cola, its value may be unknown to the company and its shareholders. Some companies include brand value as intangible assets, others do not. In the US it is not normal practice to value intangible assets unless a verifiable amount is offered for them, (thus making them tangible).

Despite this inconvenient situation, brands are assets all the same and their value to the company should be measured, not only as its sale or transfer value, but in terms of its ability to generate market pull, customers and repeat sales of goods and services. Brand owners should undertake brand audits on a regular basis. How frequently will depend on the nature of the market, how quickly it changes, how many competitors and so on. Companies who do not regularly submit their brands for a 'health check' are risking a situation where brands become damaged, outdated, pushed out of the market and eventually have a negative impact on market share. The Brand Audit Questionnaire will provide a good basis for Brand Audits.

Brand Audit Questions

- Does your company have any brands which are used to achieve prominence in the market?
- What is the value of the brand?
- What competitors does the brand have?
- Who is responsible for its management?
- List the top 3 objectives for the brand over the next twelve months
- How is this brand protected?
- What is the annual cost of protecting this brand?
- What's the relationship of this brand to its brothers and sisters?
- How is loyalty to this brand measured?
- How often is brand loyalty measured?
- How does this brand contribute to the strategic goals of the company?
- What is the synergy between the company and its brands?
- What systems are used to support brand management?
- What mechanisms are employed to ensure the continued growth and success of the brand?
- Is this a local or global brand?

WHO'S A VALUABLE CUSTOMER?

Customers are frequently lumped in to one category, but there are several types of customer which typically result from an ongoing relationship with the company and its staff. Figure 3.1 shows the stages a suspect undergoes before becoming an evangelist – the most desirable type of customer. Customers can be very expensive to acquire, depending upon the sales cycle for the product. Therefore, in order to understand the value of your customer base as an asset, it is necessary to know the sales cycle of each product or service, the cost of sales and the time it takes to convert a suspect into a customer.

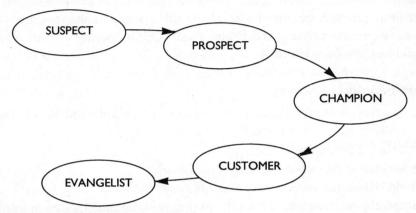

Figure 3.1 Evangelist development cycle

EVANGELIST DEVELOPMENT CYCLE

SUSPECT>>PROSPECT>>CHAMPION>>CUSTOMER>>EVANGELIST

Suspect

A suspect is a person or organization having the outward appearance of being a target for the products and services of a company. For example, if the company is selling contract accounting services, all newly established small companies would be suspects, as it would be reasonable to assume that a small company would not have the requirement for a full-time accountant and might buy in a part-time service. However, this is just a hypothesis which may be valid some of the time, but not all the time when the founder of the company happened to be a qualified accountant. Each suspect must be validated to see if they really do have a need for a particular product or service.

Prospect

Rather than try to sell to all suspects it is easier to formulate a detailed profile for a particular customer then validate the profile of each suspect to turn them in to a prospect. Such profiling vastly reduces wasted sales effort on suspects who will never become prospects for one reason or another. Incidentally, the ability to effectively profile and correctly target prospects is also an asset – an infrastructure asset which we will talk about later. If a company or individual is correctly profiled as a prospect, then the sales process is likely to be successful. Of course, there is no way of predicting events which can kill a sale: the dreaded reorganization, the prospect leaving the company, or even that the prospect just doesn't like the salesperson.

Champions

A champion is an individual inside the profiled organization who works to help the sale of an external company's products and services. Champions are desirable because they are internal agents who can influence the sale. Their motivation may be self-interest or altruism – it doesn't really matter so long as he is appropriately supported by the salesperson. The champion is a very useful person when he is working internally to help the salesperson turn a prospect into a customer.

Customers

A customer is an individual who has bought products or services. Some organizations dump customers after the sale has been made, others choose to nourish the customer relationship in the hope of turning the individual into a champion or even better, an evangelist. The customer relations strategy is largely dependent upon the nature of the product or service. Some car manufacturers follow up the purchase of a vehicle with a phone call to see if the customer is happy – nice idea. Sadly, some adopt a 'we want to know how you feel about your new car so long as everything is OK' attitude and treat sales follow up as a public relations activity.

Evangelist

An evangelist is an individual inside a customer organization who actively promotes the products and services of an external company. As with champions, their motivation may be for a variety of reasons – a dislike of the competition, a liking for small companies, a liking for an individual such as the salesperson or the Chief Executive – it doesn't really matter so long as the reason for their support is fully understood and contingency plans are put in place in the event of their support being withdrawn.

```
┌─ IC Concept#4 ──────────────────────────────────────────┐
│                                                          │
│                  Cherish Loyal Customers                 │
│                                                          │
└──────────────────────────────────────────────────────────┘
```

CUSTOMER LOYALTY

Customer loyalty is an asset, as loyalty leads to repeat business and sometimes to the existence of backlog. Measures to maintain customer loyalty vary from company to company. In consumer oriented products it's important to keep the product name constantly in the mind of the customer. Very valuable brands such as Coca-Cola and Maxwell House spend huge amounts on advertising to ensure that their market position is maintained. Other companies such as Body Shop built customer loyalty as a green company with their stance on animal testing and reusable containers. This message is reinforced on every product where the message, 'AGAINST ANIMAL TESTING', is clearly printed.

'Intel Inside'

High technology companies build customer loyalty on their innovative products and services. Intel's hugely successful 'Intel Inside' campaign was intended to build loyalty to the chip, not the computer – a novel idea which cost them dear when a mathematics professor at Lynchburg College, Virginia, discovered that his three Pentium processors were making mistakes and shared his discovery on the Internet. The problem was an obscure one, more an academic curiosity, but Intel had promoted its product as having 'unparalleled quality'. Instead of complaining to the product manufacturer, say IBM, the customers complained to Intel. Computer manufacturers must have been delighted.

Many companies don't take enough trouble to find out what would keep their customers happy; frequently it's not a lot. Information, invitations to events, even just a free glass of wine at a trade show. Having established how to gain the loyalty of the customer, follow through is essential. The launch of the NeXT computer in San Francisco comes to mind, for which a colleague received (and responded to) an RSVP invitation, made the sixty mile trip and then was turned away at the entrance by security guards as there were too many attendees.

Repeat Business

Customer loyalty is measured by repeat business and the percentage of the customer base which represents repeat business is an asset. Many industries rely on repeat business, notably airlines, insurance companies, financial services companies and so on. Skandia AFS, pioneers in the field of intellectual capital, produce an annual report on their intellectual capital which details many aspects of their IC, but notable is the attention paid to 'customer capital' as reported in their Supplement to Skandia's 1994 Annual Report.

Customer focus	1994
Market share	2.3%
Number of accounts	14,524
Customers lost	1.1%
Fund assets, excel Skandalink per customer (SEK 000)	78
Satisfied customer index (scale 1-5)	3.95

Table 3.1 Skandia's customer focus

Skandia's decision to publicize their focus on this data and improve it, is unusual and also demonstrates that they are a true third millennium company.

Customer Audit Questions
- Do we know who we are selling our products and services to?
- Do we know why customers purchase from us instead of our competitors?

- What is the potential for repeat business with our customers?
- What percentage of our customers are repeat buyers?
- What are the events which could generate repeat business?
- How do we monitor those events?
- What is the optimal time period to contact a customer?
- How often are our customers contacted?
- What activities would turn a customer into an evangelist?
- Do we have the right distribution mechanism to sell to our profiled customers?
- Are the individuals in our distribution mechanism capable of selling to our profiled customers?
- How much does it cost to make an average sale to a profiled customer?
- What is the cost to the company of losing one customer?
- What is the cost to the company of losing one market point?

DOES IT PAY TO TRACK AND MONITOR CUSTOMERS?

Yes. Information technology has revolutionized the possibilities for eager salespersons and can remind them of what they have sold to whom, who to call when and so on. Customer databases are market assets but only if they are kept up to date. The increasingly mobile work-force means that a customer database is out of date after a year. Databases also need to be constantly updated if they are to be of any value in a sales situation. Information technology can also be very seductive. The idea of one database in a company which everyone uses is appealing but not always valuable as a market asset. A database which is a collection of every person who has ever given you a business card is exactly that, not a sales database. For small and growing companies these databases can also be of use for a different reason – name recognition.

WHAT'S IN A NAME?

Company names are assets. Not only can the name itself be an asset but what it stands for in the market. This is the result of clever positioning, good public relations and word of mouth. Companies must know what their name means to customers and prospects. This information is input to marketing and public relations strategy. Without it, it's impossible to plan the strategy to either change the perception of the customer or prospect, or maintain a favourable market position.

Name Audit Questions

- What do you want your company name to mean to your prospects and customers?
- What does your company name mean to your repeat business customers?
- What does your company name mean to your one purchase customers?
- What does your company name mean to prospects who have bought from the competition instead of you?
- What does your company name mean to the financial community and investors?
- Does your company name mean the same to customers in different industries?
- Does your company name mean the same to customers in different geographical territories?

BACKLOG

Backlog is the total amount of completed sales which are due to be shipped or performed in the future. So if an organization has a service contract for £1,000,000, which will run over a two year period, that's a market asset. Because the services have not yet been performed there is a risk that something will go wrong and the contract will be lost. But with the appropriate infrastructure in place to identify and avert risk situations, backlog is an asset and mechanisms should be put in place to grow and manage backlog.

Backlog Audit Questions

- What is the average size of backlog in your company?
- What is the financial impact of having it larger or smaller?

- What is the optimum backlog for your company?
- What is the ratio of sales staff to the backlog?
- What mechanisms could be implemented to achieve optimum backlog?

IC Concept#5

Position Distribution as an Asset

PRECIOUS DISTRIBUTION

Many companies have gone to the wall with fabulous products and services because they didn't have an appropriate mechanism to get them to market. A good distribution channel is a huge asset, provided it has something to sell. Where a one-product company fails to deliver on time, or plan their product life cycle incorrectly, the company's greatest asset can be its under-utilized distribution mechanism.

There are many different distribution mechanisms – direct sales, tele-sales, retail, dealerships, the World Wide Web – the list goes on. Third millennium companies will need to find ways of getting products to market which are acceptable to customers. A sales force is a very expensive asset to establish, grow and maintain. Technology companies have led the way in finding new ways to get their products to market. There is a trend to separate product and service development and distribution. Value added resellers, which each focus on vertical markets, enable companies to pursue multiple markets in parallel without needing to become an expert on each market themselves. Software developers choose to use channels in order to keep a small tight development culture, which lends itself very well to the creative process of software development. The risk of distancing distribution from the development is a loss of contact with the customer and his needs, but this risk can be contained with good marketing and business development staff.

Distribution Audit Questions

- Upon what basis did your company choose its distribution mechanism?
- Is it appropriate for the product or service?
- How is its effectiveness measured?
- How frequently is the distribution mechanism evaluated?

- Does the distribution mechanism provide any value added services?
- What benefits does your chosen distribution mechanism have over other options?
- What is the ROI for the distribution mechanism?
- Would your company gain any benefit from having external distribution mechanisms?
- List 10 changes you would make to the operation of the distribution mechanism.
- List 10 reasons why those changes have not been made.

BUSINESS COLLABORATIONS

Organizations which decide to get their products to market via external distribution channels must be able to collaborate with their partners. The ability to collaborate easily is an asset as it enables partners to come together to pursue a business opportunity which they would not have been able to pursue independently. Understanding what makes a collaboration successful is important. All companies are different and knowing the limitations of the partners is essential. It is worthwhile auditing the last half dozen collaborations undertaken by your company to see if there is any trend towards successful or unsuccessful collaboration. Over the past three years The Technology Broker has audited 80 collaborations undertaken by one of its clients and the number one reason a collaboration may not be as successful as they had originally hoped, is clashing corporate cultures – more about that later.

Collaboration Audit Questions

- Does your company evaluate build or buy options when developing new products and services?
- How does your company track and identify opportunities to collaborate with partners?
- Can you identify a consistent weakness in some operating function in the company?
- How many collaborations has your company participated in over the last two years?

- How many were successful?
- Of those which were not successful, what was the main reason for their failure?

FRANCHISE AGREEMENTS

When we think of franchise we typically think of McDonalds or dry cleaning companies, but that's not necessarily what they are restricted to. The British Franchise Association publishes this lengthy but complete definition of the franchise:

> A contractual license granted by one person (the franchisor) to another (the franchisee) which:
> (a) permits or requires the franchisee to carry on during the period of the franchise, a particular business under or using a specific name belonging to or associated with the franchisor; and
> (b) entitles the franchisor to provide the franchisee with assistance in carrying on the business which is the subject of the franchise; and
> (c) obliges the franchisor to provide the franchisee with assistance in carrying out the business which is the subject of the franchise (in relation to the organization of the franchisee's business, the training of staff, merchandising management or otherwise); and
> (d) requires the franchisee periodically during the period of the franchise, to pay the franchisor sums of money in consideration for the franchise, or for goods or services provided by the franchisor for the franchisee; and
> (e) which is not a transaction between subsidiaries of the same holding company, or between subsidiaries of the same holding company, or between an individual and a company controlled by him.
>
> *The British Franchise Association*

Franchising is an attractive option when the business opportunity can be described by way of a clearly defined formula. This formula is typically written down and becomes the operating manual for new franchisees. The value of a franchise will depend upon a number of factors, notably branding customer loyalty to the franchise and a sound financial track record of early franchisees.

The ability to franchise a business is therefore an asset, as it enables inorganic growth of a single named entity without costly investment in organic growth.

Coca-Cola, Pepsi and 7-Up

Coca-Cola, Pepsi and 7-Up are all products which require large quantities of water, which makes transport from central locations very costly. Coca-Cola, Pepsi and 7-Up all used franchising as a means of expansion. Franchisees bought concentrated drink syrup and made the product at their own bottling plants, distributing it to local markets.

LICENSING AGREEMENTS

Licensing agreements encompass wide ranging agreements which give one party the right to sell your products, services or technology to other parties in accordance with the conditions as set out in the agreement. Many organizations do not pursue opportunities to license into markets other than their own as they feel they don't have the time or expertise to set up the arrangement. This can mean that a huge amount of potential revenue for the company never materializes. There are ways of averting this undesirable situation. The organization can appoint a business development manager whose function is to identify and pursue licensing opportunities on behalf of the company. Alternatively, organizations can use a third party which specializes in seeking out favourable licensing agreements. This strategy is particularly attractive when organizations have developed technology, methods and so on for themselves, but there are many wide ranging, non-competitive relationships they can enter in to with partners in different markets.

FAVOURABLE CONTRACTS

A favourable contract is one which has been obtained by a company because of some unique market position they hold. Examples might be spare parts for a particular machine which no one else could supply, or cut-rate advertising due to the buying power of some of the world's biggest spenders on advertising. Such contracts are clearly a competitive advantage, but they are also market assets.

CAN MARKET-CENTRED ASSETS ACHIEVE CORPORATE GOALS?

Having lots of market assets is great, but only if they either contribute towards achieving corporate goals, or can be sold off at a profit. Understanding the corporate goals is the number one priority when attempting to assess the intellectual capital of the organization, because market assets which lack synergy will ultimately give a confusing picture to the market and its customers, resulting in a weakening of the company's position in the market-place.

So, despite the fact that the company may have some great market assets, unless they can be used to achieve corporate goals and strengthen the company, they should be disposed of.

INSUFFICIENT MARKET ASSETS TO ACHIEVE CORPORATE GOALS?

Should the company find the cupboard a bit bare when examining its market assets, the first job is to identify the holes and brainstorm the best possible scenario which would fix the situation. There are a number of ways in which market assets can be generated. Before acquiring market assets from outside the company it is best to take a good look at why market assets are missing. This is achieved by undertaking a market asset audit which we talk about later. Once that is complete a strategy to increase market assets can be designed, together with a tactical plan to implement it.

Summary of Market-centred Assets

- Service brands
- Product brands
- Corporate brands

- Champions
- Customers
- Evangelists
- Customer loyalty
- Repeat business
- Company name
- Backlog
- Distribution channels
- Business collaborations
- Franchise agreements
- Licensing agreements
- Favourable contracts

4

Intellectual Property Assets

Intellectual property (IP) is a form of property – protected in law – which is derived from the mind. The term usually refers to patent, copyright, trade marks, trade secrets, proprietary technology and know-how. Intellectual property law may vary from country to country but its generic attributes are described below.

PATENT

A patent is a property right which is granted by the state to its inventor. The right is exclusive, which means that the owner has a monopoly for a period of time and the right to exclude others from making, copying or selling the invention. In order for a patent to be granted, the invention must be disclosed or put into the public domain. The advantage of this is that it provides a 'Keep Off' sign on the invention, which is clearly defined. The disadvantage of publication is that it is no longer a secret.

Ownership of a patent can be very valuable, but only if the owner is active not passive. It should be noted that a patent is a right and the owner has to assert that right. If the owner does not assert his rights, others will infringe his rights with impunity. With new products organizations sometimes choose to protect the project with multiple patents, one for each component or part – referred to as a thicket. For example, the Kodak Instamatic camera was protected by a thicket of patents consisting of more than a hundred individual filings, making the product very difficult for Kodak's competitors to copy.

Should a company choose to license its invention to other companies, revenue generated from the licensing agreement is a market asset, as explained in the previous chapter. In order to have value, a patent must be exploited and defended. Organizations which do not pursue infringement of their patent are not only leaving money on the table from uncollected royalties, they are also devaluing their own intellectual property asset. Cynics would say that a patent is only as valuable as the amount of money its owner is prepared to spend defending it. To some extent this is true, as evidenced by the huge amounts of money spent on protecting valuable patents. A patent for its own sake has no point or value.

Altruistic inventors may choose not to patent, but put their invention into the public domain for all to share. This fine deed sometimes has the opposite effect, as without a guaranteed monopoly companies may choose not to invest in commercialization of an invention, as they risk losing their investment to a better competitor. This was allegedly the case with penicillin, whose inventor Alexander Fleming chose not to patent it, delaying its introduction to the market as a drug because companies were loath to invest in its productization.

Ownership of a patent portfolio is only an asset when it is managed properly. Perhaps a patent is sought, but never used, in order to prevent a competitor from bringing a new product to market. Perhaps a patent has been sought to protect an investment in commercialization of an invention, such as a drug. In both cases infringement must be contested for the patent to have value.

Patents can also lull an organization into a false sense of security, as the revenue which is derived from a patent may eventually cease when the patent lapses and copies are permitted. Patents are potentially very valuable assets, provided they are appropriately managed.

┌─ IC Concept#6 ──────────────────────────────────────┐
│   │
│   Patents Protect Profits   │
│   │
└──┘

Patent Audit Questions

- How many patents does your organization own?
- What is the major reason for filing patents?
- How is the production of patents linked to corporate goals?
- Who is responsible for determining protection policies for patents?
- How much does your organization spend on patent protection each year?
- What is your company's ROI on the patents it owns?
- To what extent are the patents owned by your company optimally exploited?
- Does your company have a patent policy which helps you determine whether intellectual property should be protected via patent or as a trade secret?
- Are your scientists familiar with the basics of intellectual property law?

COPYRIGHT

Copyright protects the expression of an idea, not the idea itself. Protection commences when the expression is fixed in some tangible form, such as when it is written down. In some countries, for example the USA, copyright may be registered. The duration of copyright protection may vary from country to country, but in general it is for the life of the author plus at least fifty years. Copyright protection is generally given to literary works, motion pictures, choreographic works, pictorial, graphic and sculptural works and musical works. In addition, computer software can be protected by copyright.

Copyright is an asset as the work can be sold, distributed or licensed, generating wealth for its owner. Examples include books, where the author may give a publisher permission to publish, market and sell the work in return for a royalty fee.

Copyright Audit Questions

- What aspects of your company's business are protected by copyright?
- Does your company build computer software?
- Is there any stronger protection which could be used to protect software, such as patent?
- Are your employees aware of the basics of copyright protection?
- What action does your company take to ensure that its copyright is not violated?
- What copyrights owned by your company are of value?

DESIGNS

The protection of designs varies between countries, so it's important to know the situation as products and services are sold from country to country. Different protection can be sought in different countries. For example, in the UK designs can be protected in two ways – registered designs and design rights. A registered design, or design patent, is a monopoly for the outward appearance of an article or a set of articles of manufacture to which the design is applied. It protects the novelty of the design which has 'eye appeal'. A design right protects the original design or shape of an article and gives the owner the right to prevent any one else from copying it. As the United Kingdom is part of the European Community, whose aim is to harmonize intellectual property law throughout Europe, we anticipate some movement within Europe on some of these issues.

Design Audit Questions

- What aspects of your company's products could be protected via one of the design rights?
- Would a design right give your company a competitive advantage in some area?
- Are your product designers all familiar with benefits of protection afforded by design rights?

TRADE MARKS

A trade mark is a registered mark which is associated with a company or its products, which distinguishes them from those owned by others. The mark can be a word such as a name, a stylized name, a picture or a logo or a combination. Exclusive rights to trade marks are obtained by continual use and may be registered by the Patent Office. Trade marks are used to protect brands and can become very valuable assets which live for a long time, increasing in value over the years.

SERVICE MARKS

A service mark is similar to a trade mark, except it is used to distinguish the services of one company from another. Like trade marks, service marks can be registered and exclusive rights assigned to those which are registered and in continual use.

TRADE SECRETS

A trade secret is a piece of information which is not known within the trade. It can be an unpatented invention, a piece of news, a new invention, a process and so on. Trade secrets are protected by confidentiality or non-disclosure agreements which should state the term of the agreement and the conditions under which the secret must be kept. Sometimes companies will choose to keep a formula or process as a trade secret to avoid publishing it in a patent. In order to determine if the best protection is trade secret or patent, the risk of the patent being challenged or infringed must be weighed against the risk of the secret becoming public.

Trade Secret Audit Questions
- Under what circumstances are trade secret or confidentiality agreements entered in to in your company?
- Who is authorized to sign trade secret agreements within your company?
- Are your staff aware that they are signing to keep trade secrets on behalf of the company not themselves?
- Where are trade secret agreements kept in your company?

KNOW-HOW

Know-how refers to the body of knowledge individuals possess about a particular topic. Knowledge may be quite straight forward to explain, for example, how to raise a purchase order or it might be deep, such as how to design aeroplane wings. It also may be tacit – which means that it is difficult to articulate – such as what a good wine smells like or the consistency of a new margarine which will successfully scale up for mass production. Researchers in artificial intelligence have been examining issues related to computer representation of all forms of knowledge for quite some time. Although there are some computer systems which exhibit knowledgeable performance in a variety of applications, know-how still remains the property of the individual. For this reason we expand on know-how in our discussion of human-centred assets.

HOW DO IP ASSETS CONTRIBUTE TOWARDS CORPORATE GOALS?

Undertaking an intellectual property audit is not a new idea, as most companies need to be aware of the patents and designs they own in order to manage appropriate protection. However, the intellectual property department in the majority of corporations has a protection function and is not proactive from a business perspective. After all, knowing that you own a patent is not a lot of use if that fact is not accompanied with information concerning its potential. This is evaluated from the various aspects that the patent can be viewed from including: return on investment, commercial potential, competitive advantage and so on. It is important to note that intellectual property assets should not just be considered from their legal perspective, they should also should mirror that raison d'être.

What's a Xerox?

Pick ten people at random. Ask them 'What's a Xerox?' most will answer 'a copy machine'. Yet if any one of those people is a computer person they might answer 'The place where the best computer lab in the world is', or 'a failed computer system'. True, Xerox does have a highly reputable computer lab. And they did bring to the market in the early eighties a remarkable machine with windows, icons, pretty much what you'd expect to see today from Microsoft Windows or the Apple Macintosh. Although they had this technology on the market before all of their eventual competitors the machine never really made it. Why? Not because it wasn't a great machine, because it was, but because Xerox is a copy machine company, not a computer company. Years later companies such as Sun Microsystems, Apple and eventually Microsoft, exploited similar technology and dominated the market because it was their core business; it wasn't Xerox's. The best intellectual property on the planet doesn't generate revenue if the company is not correctly positioned to exploit it. In the third millennium we will see increasing use of computers to manipulate information. An increase in electronic transmission and digital publication of information has no doubt had an influence on Xerox's positioning strategy. Now they are 'the Document Company' paper, electronic whatever.

┌─ IC Concept#7 ─────────────────────────────────

Intellectual Property is a Corporate Investment

Summary of Intellectual Property Assets

- Patent
- Copyright
- Design rights
- Trade secrets
- Know-how
- Trade marks
- Service marks

5
Human-centred Assets

Joe was just finishing his presentation to the Client, when he noticed the Client was peering at the business cards he and his two colleagues had presented.

'How come you guys don't have any titles on your business cards' asked the Client.

'Well', said Joe cautiously, 'we are a small company, just 15 people and we all do many things – we have to respond to the client's needs, we have no set job titles.'

'Yeah', said the Client pensively, 'yeah'.

As they left the building Joe walked briskly to the car, 'Damn', he said, 'They won't give us the business because they think we're too small, I can't wait until we get bigger.'

The Client had lunch with his boss.

'Next time we get business cards printed I think we should leave the titles off.' 'Why?' asked the boss. 'Because that would help get rid of this notion that the employee just did the job, rather than whatever the client wanted or the company needed. Let me tell you about this smart little company I met today…'

WHO ARE THE PEOPLE WE WORK WITH?

The people we work with are largely unknown to us. Although they spend a huge proportion of their time at work, we see only a few aspects of their capabilities. This is typically because they come labelled with job titles, restricting their contribution to the organization as a whole. We stick labels on people's foreheads, put them in jobs and leave them there, ignoring all other contributions they could make to the company. It's saying that the environment they work in (and therefore their job) is static – it isn't.

THE THIRD MILLENNIUM WORK-FORCE

The third millennium work-force is a knowledge based work-force. It emanates from a population that lives longer and demands a higher quality of life than its predecessors. There will be fewer 'jobs' and a larger number of people wanting employment. Workers won't necessarily come to a place of work each day, instead working from home or at a client site as the project requires. The work-force is participatory, understanding the goals of the company and receiving satisfaction from knowing the part they play in achieving them. The culture in the organization is different from fifty years ago. It's changed from being authoritative to participative. Before, it was more formal, hierarchical, powerful from the top, with distant management. In the third millennium company the emphasis is on sharing, encouraging involvement and empowerment, showing an appreciation for individuals' contributions in the organization.

THE MEDIA MANIPULATES THE MARKET

The market changes faster now than ever before. It will become a lot more dynamic. The media web which spans the entire planet has meant that customers are more informed about the products and services they buy than ever before. Customers don't just want products for their own sake, they care about how they are made, who makes them and the impact their methods of production have on the environment. Consider dolphin-friendly tuna. Twenty years ago there was no demand for it. The media web which publicized the cruelty to dolphins by some tuna fishing fleet didn't exist then. But the use of media by concerned individuals created a demand for a dolphin-friendly product. Almost overnight the product was born, forcing competitors to follow suit within weeks. To stay afloat in a global market the ability to change quickly and respond to market needs is essential.

Our Jobs Have Gone Forever

So what's the impact of the ever changing market on our jobs? The traditional notion of employment is that companies advertise for a set of abilities and experience, set them out in a job specification, then review employee performance against the specification, say, twice a year. That was fine when the 'job' was static. The reality of today and the future is that by the time the employee joins the company the market demand may have changed, so the job has either gone away or changed. Maybe the new employee can't do the new job – they're redundant before their new business cards arrive. Employers have increasingly rigorous labour legislation to adhere to. This makes the notion of hiring an individual for a 'job' a really scary prospect. So something has to change, and it's the way we think about employment.

Focus on Getting on Not Getting Up

As kids we are taught to respect our elders and superiors and to aspire to get to the top. We talk about our colleagues and friends as having a really 'good job'. But as we have seen in the recession of the 1990s, good jobs with their high salaries, cars and privileges can vanish overnight. During the previous three decades the drive to get to the top dominated the mind of many employees. Although many were promoted, they did not become more valuable to the organization – just more expensive. So when times got hard and the organization considered employee value, they had to go. The removal of middle management is also a reflection of a global culture shift in organizations from authoritative to participative. Middle managers slowed down or even blocked the required transition. They represented the old way. Employees must now focus on getting on, not getting up. They need to understand where the market, and therefore the company, is going. They need to be able to see how they can best help the organization respond to market needs.

RESPONDING TO MARKET NEEDS

To stay competitive, organizations must respond to market needs. That means that products and services must respond to that pull too. Much delivered by third millennium companies will be by way of products and services which are delivered by people. Those who help the organization satisfy customer needs become valuable assets. The value of those who don't quickly diminishes. Valuable human assets are those which can support the organization and respond to market pull. When the company becomes misaligned with its market and market pull is diminishing, valuable human assets are those which are able to generate new strategies, products, services and technologies which are able to push the market.

Human-centred Asset Audit Questions

- What percentage of employees in your company are actually doing the job they were originally hired to do?
- What percentage of your employees could accurately state the corporate goals for the current financial year?
- How do employees in your company know at the end of each day that they have made a worthwhile contribution to the company?
- How do employees know when there is a need in your company so they can contribute to filling that need?
- How are employees made aware of what is happening in the market your company operates in?

THINKING ABOUT PEOPLE

There are many ways in which to think about people when trying to assess their value, both current and potential to the organization. We refer to these different views as 'aspects'. It is possible to spend a huge amount of time in trying to design a common set of aspects which will satisfy the needs of all organizations, that is not our goal. We outline the basic set which enables those involved in intellectual capital management to begin the audit process and design new aspects which they add to their taxonomy to suit their businesses. The categories we recommend to begin with are as follows and are discussed below.

- Education
- Vocational qualifications
- Work related knowledge
- Occupational assessments and psychometrics
- Work related competencies

It must be stressed that the aspects of the individual which are of interest to the organization will vary from company to company and from time to time. Also, the individual will grow and change, not only as a result of education and acquisition of new skills, but also because they just get older and more experienced and their personality profiles may change a bit as a result of life experiences. This means that any audit exercise in management of human-centred assets must be continuous.

EDUCATION

Education refers to the formal education a person would have had at an educational establishment between the ages of four and sixteen to eighteen and is not to be confused with vocational qualifications which are described below. Education does not prepare the individual for any job in particular. Examples of education include:

- All methods of communicating via language
- Mathematics
- Physics
- Chemistry
- History
- Geography
- Problem solving
- Artistic and creative pursuits
- Basic socialization

An 'education' is basically the bedrock upon which other aspects of the individual can be built. Tertiary education increases the level of education, but its primary goal is not usually vocational.

Audit Questions About Employee Education
- Can you characterize the mix of educational background best suited to particular job functions in your company?
- To what extent is it necessary to supplement the education of employees once they have joined the company?
- How are employees made aware that additional education would improve their job performance?
- How are employees made aware that additional education would have direct impact on their remuneration?
- Does your company give any advice or counselling to employees on educational issues?

VOCATIONAL QUALIFICATIONS

Vocational qualifications are based on what an individual does in the workplace. They are intended to allow the individual to prove that they have the skills, knowledge and understanding to do a job well. These skills are verified in a number of ways from examination to continual assessment. Vocational qualifications can be gained in a wide variety of fields including:

- Travel
- Computing
- Decoration
- Management
- Mechanical engineering
- Retail operations
- Management

Throughout the world, vocational qualifications have been designed, monitored and managed by trade and professional bodies for decades; it's an on-going process. For employers this can be a problem – not knowing what a qualification represents in different skills from different teaching establishments, makes it hard to compare qualifications. As the work-force becomes more global, this problem is magnified as there are no international standards.

┌─ IC Concept#8 ─────────────────────────────────┐

Valuable Employers and Employees Invest in Themselves

└───┘

The National Vocational Qualification System

In 1988 the British Government set up the National Council for Vocational Qualifications. Its goal was to develop, implement, monitor and promote a comprehensive system of vocational qualifications in England, Wales and Northern Ireland. The NCVQ worked together with existing organizations, who already designed and managed vocational training, in order to establish a uniform framework which represented levels of competence as outlined by employers in a wide range of business sectors.

The primary purposes of the NVQ framework as outlined in their magazine *Monitor* are: 'to create a coherent classification for qualifications and to facilitate transfer and progression, both within areas of competence and between them'. The system uses four levels of competence in the performance of a range of varied work activities:

- Level 1: competence in the performance of a range of varied work activities, most of which may be routine and predictable.

- Level 2: competence in a significant range of varied work activities, performed in a variety of contexts. Some of the activities are complex or non-routine and there is some individual responsibility or autonomy. Collaboration with others, perhaps through membership of a work group or team, may often be a requirement.

- Level 3: Competence in a broad range of varied work activities performed in a wide variety of contexts and most of which are complex and non-routine. There is considerable responsibility and autonomy and control or guidance of others is often required.

- Level 4: competence in a broad range of complex, technical or professional work activities performed in a wide variety of contexts and with a substantial personal responsibility and autonomy.

Responsibility for the work of others and the allocation of resources is often present.

- Level 5: competence which involves the application of a significant range of fundamental principles and complex techniques across a wide and often unpredictable variety of contexts. Very substantial personal autonomy and often significant responsibility for the work of others (and for the allocation of substantial resources) feature strongly, as do personal accountabilities for analysis and diagnosis, design, planning, execution and evaluation.

The system was not intended to create new courses, but to standardize existing ones and set a standard for the design of future programmes. So individuals who already have a degree in, say, mechanical engineering could, if they wished, have that qualification verified in terms of an NVQ. It's also important to note that the NVQ system is about demonstrating competence, so the practical aspects of the job are the focus and exams are not common.

So far there are 135 awarding bodies who are responsible for over 800 NVQs in a wide range of industries. By June 1995 a total of 885,264 NVQ certificates had been awarded. The British NVQ system is not unique, with similar schemes under way in other countries. Such schemes give us a framework to think about some of our human-centred assets.

Vocational Qualification Audit Questions

- To what extent are vocational qualifications formally recognized in your company?
- How do your employees know when it is time to learn new vocational skills?
- Who is responsible for determining if the work-force has the vocational qualifications to satisfy corporate goals?
- Is there a policy for re-educating the work-force with new vocational skills?
- How are employees made aware of a shift in vocational skill requirement so they can opt for retraining in time to contribute towards the achievement of corporate goals?

WORK RELATED KNOWLEDGE

Work related knowledge is knowledge which frequently comes as a function of understanding and doing a job in a particular field. It comprises three types of knowledge: tacit, explicit and implicit.

Tacit Knowledge

Tacit knowledge is knowledge which exists and can be used by individuals, but is extremely difficult to explain or write down. When knowledge elicitors are working with individuals who are rich in tacit knowledge, early questions concerning their special ability are typically returned with a glazed look and a response of 'Well, I just know'. One client was concerned that there were only two individuals in the company who could tell when an experimental quantity of a new margarine would successfully scale up for mass production – by just looking at it. They were dismayed to discover that they were unable to teach anybody else the skill, despite apprentices following them about all day watching what they were doing. The alternative, when the experts resigned and the apprentices took over, was huge wastage as they determined what would scale up and what wouldn't through trial and error. If documenting and recording tacit knowledge is difficult, which it is, it is essential for the organization to know who has what tacit knowledge and ensure that they are treated as the valuable asset they really are. Such valuable assets are always in demand by competitors and if not nurtured may vanish. Ill conceived re-engineering programmes can remove valuable assets in this way.

Explicit Knowledge

Explicit knowledge can readily be written down. It is well organized in the mind of the individual and may also be written down in books, manuals, procedures and so forth. Examples of explicit knowledge would include the operating manual for a franchise where all of the operating knowledge concerning the franchise must be written down and transferred to the franchisee by definition.

Implicit Knowledge

Implicit knowledge is knowledge which is hidden in the operating procedures, methods and even the corporate culture of the company. As they are hidden they are difficult for the novice or beginner to identify and therefore learn.

Individuals in possession of such knowledge are thought of as experts. To the non-expert they seem to have magic in their fingers and know all sorts of clever tricks and short cuts they use in order to get the job done. These are the guys that you call in when traditional methods don't work. Identifying and transferring this type of knowledge from one person to another can be very difficult as quite frequently the individual is unable to explain why they know that a certain process works. Working with experts to gather and document this type of knowledge is called knowledge elicitation. It is a technique which began in the early 1980s in order to collect expert knowledge which could then be used to build expert systems. Expert systems are computer systems which emulate the problem solving technique and knowledge of a human expert.

┌─ IC Concept#9 ──┐

Knowledge Rich Employees Add Value

└──┘

Expert Systems

Expert systems have been built for over twenty years now. They tend to be very effective when the problem space, or domain, is limited and well defined. For example, when diagnosing faults in railway track and choosing a course of action to fix the track, it's possible to build a brick wall around that domain. Whereas building an expert system to schedule air flight crews is a lot more difficult as there are so many constraints to the problem, many of which are external, so building a wall around the problem is much more difficult. However, expert systems are of great interest to those who are seeking to identify and disseminate expertise throughout the work-force. Although there are many types of knowledge which are unsuitable for expert systems at this time and should remain in the domain of researchers, there are also numerous applications which are appropriate.

Work Related Knowledge Audit Questions

- On what special knowledge does your company depend to operate?
- Where are those knowledge assets within the company?
- Can they be easily identified?
- Can those assets be easily described?
- Is there any way in which those assets can be transferred to another employee?
- What methods does your company use to disseminate those assets within the company?
- Would those assets be valuable to a competitor?
- How are those assets protected on behalf of your company?
- If these assets were lost to your company how would they be replaced?
- Would their loss have any impact on the effective operation of the company?
- Could they be replaced?
- What would be the cost of replacing them?

OCCUPATIONAL ASSESSMENT AND PSYCHOMETRICS

Occupational assessment refers to a wide range of objective assessment, psychometric testing and personality profiling which is done via testing methods. Typically used in order to support the selection process when hiring new employees, these tests are under-utilized when looking for ways of thinking about people. In general, psychometric tests have a negative profile. Many of us associate them with intelligence tests we were given in our adolescence which used to tell us that we were suitable to be a nurse, or a lab technician, when those were the last occupations on the planet we saw ourselves doing for the rest of our lives. Today, the portfolio of tests is a lot more sophisticated, giving both the individual and the organization new and stimulating ways to think about people, their potential and the ways they may work within the organization. Aptitude tests address a wide range from low skills to complex decision making processes. Examples include:

- Advanced management tests
- Critical reasoning tests

- Information technology aptitudes
- Customer contact
- Personnel
- Mechanical comprehension
- Automated office
- Selling skills
- Technical skills
- Manual dexterity
- Occupational interest
- Career guidance
- Modern languages

and many many more.

Other tests focus on personality profiles and motivation:
- Team types, leaders, subordinate styles etc.
- Selling and influencing styles
- Critical thinking
- Personal integrity
- Objective personality, initiative, tenacity, drive etc.
- Perspectives – how individuals are seen by others
- Self-perception versus those of a boss, subordinate, colleague and so on
- Thinking styles
- Work styles
- Motivation factors

Boxes and Pigeon-holes

The use of occupational assessment and personality tests is widespread in industry but they could become significantly more beneficial if their use was expanded. For example, a person may join a company as a technician be tested to validate their appointment to the job and hired. However, they might have the potential to become a super salesperson, it just never occurred to the individual that sales was an option. Once pigeon-holed as a technician, the move into the sales organization might be quite hard, so they are stuck. A better approach would be to give an individual a range of tests and continue the process so that both the individual and the organization have the opportunity to look at the whole individual, not just the part which featured most prominently in the job ad.

Occupational Assessment Audit Questions
- What percentage of employees in your company have undertaken any form of occupational assessment?
- Was the purpose to evaluate the potential of the individual?
- Is occupational assessment used in your company for any reason other than recruiting?
- Are personality tests given in your company?
- How is information generated from personality tests used in your company?
- Who is responsible for giving such tests?
- How is test data shared with appropriate people?
- Are such tests viewed as a positive or negative activity?

The Individual is a Big Secret

Because of the stigma so many of us have about all forms of testing, we are usually disinclined to share information about ourselves which may be really helpful in the workplace. Using personality profiles as the basis for discussing problems in the workplace can be a revelation for individuals who have a problem understanding why colleagues behave in particular ways. Sometimes problems which have dogged us for years just melt away when we understand more about our colleagues' perspective. In addition, teams dominated by several individuals with the same personality type may need to be balanced by others with different personality attributes.

WORK RELATED COMPETENCIES

NVQ type systems provide a sound foundation and will continue to grow over future years, but the organization requires more specific information on the abilities of its employees. It needs to know how vocational qualifications, work related knowledge and personality profiles come together and are used within the context of its own business. Can an individual back up a computer system or design a marketing strategy for that particular company? In addition, an employee may have acquired 'on the job knowledge' which is patchy with respect to an NVQ system, but none the less useful to the organization. Finally, there may be some skills developed specifically by the organization for the organization, proprietary methods and so on. We call these aspects workplace competencies and they tend to be at a higher level of abstraction than previous aspects, as they frequently combine them.

Human assets that can push and respond to market pull have a desirable set of work related competencies. Work related competencies can best be thought of as a merged set of skills, creative profiles, personality attributes and vocational qualifications. Examples of work related competencies include:

- The ability to design a marketing strategy in Company X
- The ability to value an asset in Company X
- The ability to operate a machine in Company X
- The ability to manage a project in Company X
- The ability to speak a foreign language in Company X
- The ability to work well in a team in Company X
- The ability to teach a subject in Company X
- The ability to sell a particular product in Company X

By focussing on work related competencies instead of jobs, teams of individuals can be pulled together or disbanded in order to suit a client need or an emerging market situation. Work related competencies are not static. The performance of a task for a company is a means of growing a workplace competency. Clearly, employees who develop work related competencies in doing things they like will be happier (and no doubt perform better) delivering a better service to the customer.

Viewing the work-force as a pool of work related competencies has other desirable attributes. The organization needs to be able to share with its employees the skills and competencies at all levels it perceives it needs into the future. Companies with good market research and strategic planning capabilities can also predict the future requirements of the work-force. Where there is a fit that's great. Where there isn't there is the opportunity to acquire the capability organically or inorganically.

Work Related Competency Audit Questions

- Pick an important function in your company – what work related competencies does that function require?
- What work related competencies will it require next year?
- Are staff already in place to respond to the change?
- Are resources in place to fill the gap?
- How long will it take to fill the gap?
- What will be the cost implications of that gap?
- How are work related competencies planned for the future?
- Is the employee able to acquire the competence via training?

ORGANIC VERSUS INORGANIC GROWTH

Organic growth of competencies requires a partnership between the employee and the company where the employee agrees to train to acquire a competency required by the company. How this manifests itself within corporate training programmes will vary from one organization to another. There are two requirements for the success of this approach:

1 Communication of corporate goals by the company to the employee so that they can make an informed choice of whether or not to invest personal resources in acquiring the new competency. It's not possible for the employee to plan a journey if they don't know where they're going.

2 The employee must take ownership and responsibility for developing a set of competencies and understand that the organization will hold them accountable to deliver them. In return, competencies become bargaining chips with which remuneration can be agreed.

Inorganic growth of work related competencies means that they will be acquired from outside the company. In some circumstances this will be desirable. For example, where the competency is short-term or is highly specialized such as the traditional use of professional services or the need for an individual who possesses a particular knowledge. Where the need is long-term the organization has to weigh up the risk of bringing in a new individual and the time it takes them to become assimilated into the corporate culture so that they are able to perform, versus the learning curve for organic growth.

┌─ IC Concept#10 ──┐

Protect and Grow Core Competencies

└───┘

Falling into the Competency Chasm

Employees who do not audit and maintain their competencies risk falling into a competency chasm, which can ultimately lead to lifelong unemployment. To avoid this situation individuals must seek associations with organizations which will give them valuable advice and feedback on their competencies so that they know how to plan for their own future and security. To do nothing has the same impact as ignoring the maintenance of any other valuable asset – it devalues and gets put on the list to go.

Motivation and Empowerment

John F Kennedy moved his entire nation when he said 'Ask not what your country can do for you – but what you can do for your country'. Employees should perhaps ask themselves the same question about their company. There is a mind shift which must take place within the workforce in order for them to accept the reality of companies equipped to operate in the third millennium. Those who make the transition will be motivated and become empowered, increasing their value to the organization. Valuable employees are needed more by the company than they need it.

Self-managed Learning

In the third millennium, knowledge is the single most important asset and we should spend a sizable proportion of our time on maintaining the greatest asset we have during our life. Yet most of us spend more on clothes or car maintenance than education, training and the acquisition of new knowledge. The mind set fostered throughout the second millennium was that it's someone elses' responsibility to plan and pay for our personal growth – parents, education, the state, the employer. One huge

US company recently announced that it paid for an average of five days per annum on staff development and training per employee. It's not enough. Conventional teaching methods are too expensive for companies to invest in thirty to sixty days per annum. Fortunately in the third millennium we will have access to a phenomenal range of learning mechanisms right inside our own homes via the Internet, our TV and computer. We will be able to customize self-managed learning programmes ourselves. The amount we are able to learn will be limited only by our own desire. Self-managed learning does not have to be a lonely experience, it's richer if done in partnership with the organization which can give advice and feedback to the individual.

Corporate Learning Audit Questions

- Who designs corporate learning programmes in your company?
- How are the goals of the company fed into corporate learning?
- What is the average length of time that knowledge in your company is current and useful?
- What percentage of employees are 'in learning' at any one time?
- How are employees incentivised to participate in learning programmes?
- How does the organization recognize those who do participate in learning?
- Are employees encouraged to read books, journals and other material relevant to your business at work?
- Does your company have a library in every facility?
- Are employees made aware of new books, papers and reports in the library?
- Does senior management participate in employee training, attend courses their employees attend?

An Attitude About People – East versus West

In his book *Made in Japan; Akio Morita & Sony* Akio Morita, one of the founders of Sony, comments on the differences in philosophy between Japan and the West with respect to managing an employee who is not performing in his job. In the US the individual is typically seen as a failure and is fired. In Japan, the manager is seen as a failure and seeks to find the right job for the individual within the organization. This difference is also reflected in the investment Japan puts into its employees. They invest for life and develop long range strategies which give them the space to develop employees in harmony with their strategies. This long-term commitment to both employee and strategy is one of the great strengths which enabled Japan to become a leading industrial player in the seventies and eighties. In the West we tend to be a lot more reactive to the feast-famine cycle – hiring when times are good, firing when they're bad. Massive sums of money are wasted as we hire, train, absorb into the culture then fire. In order to understand the nature of human-centred assets within the corporation it is necessary to examine the different aspects of employees.

---IC Concept#11 ----------------

Manage Human Resources

HUMAN-CENTRED ASSET MANAGEMENT

We have talked about the different aspects individuals can be viewed from and it can be a very complex business. The management process is frequently fed via a three-way process and includes peer-to-peer review, manager and reportee review. It is also designed to be open between the individual and his manager, as the method encourages empowerment of the individual. In addition, it enhances his knowledge of the organization's goals as well as where and how he can best contribute to the successful attainment of those goals to mutual benefit.

Skills traditionally kept inside human resource departments must be spread throughout the company, or the role of the human resources professional repositioned within the company to support the needs of line managers. Human resource professionals in the third millennium need to be able to view the organization as a dynamic entity and seek out ways of assisting management to understand the nature of human-centred assets they have already in employment, how to develop those assets for the future and locate the missing pieces of the jigsaw.

Human-centred Asset Management Audit Questions
• Where in your company will human-centred assets be managed?

- What is the optimal number of individuals a manager can effectively manage?
- What role will the Human Resources department play in this process?

CAN HUMAN-CENTRED ASSETS ACHIEVE CORPORATE GOALS?

The final, most important question is can human-centred assets achieve corporate goals? Many organizations can't answer this question as they don't really understand the nature of the employees they pay each month and sometimes the corporate goals as well. It seems silly to consider setting up an international transport business with bicycles and pushcarts and two trucks, or planning to buy a building with no money for electricity or maintenance, but that's the behaviour some companies exhibit. No organization could say that it had exactly the right human resource in place at the right time with the right skill optimally used – otherwise we would be using more than 20% of our employees' capability. There's lots of room for improvement.

Summary of Human-centred Assets
- Education
- Vocational qualifications
- Work related knowledge
- Occupational assessments
- Psychometrics
- Work related competencies

6
Infrastructure Assets

Infrastructure assets are the skeleton and glue of the organization, they provide strength and cohesion between its people and its processes. Without a strong infrastructure companies deliver products and services of poor quality and the employees are frequently disheartened and disoriented. Corporate infrastructure is comprised of the following elements:

- Management philosophy
- Corporate culture
- Management processes
- Information technology systems
- Networking systems
- Financial relations

MANAGEMENT PHILOSOPHY

Management philosophy is the way company leaders think about their company and its employees and has a dominant effect on corporate culture. Management philosophies change with the times and reflect themselves in how individuals are managed and motivated. The company management philosophy can be custom, reflecting the philosophy of key leaders, such as the Hewlett Packard philosophy which has been quoted as an all-American values philosophy. Companies may have management philosophies which are out of tune with the times and are not assets, but liabilities.

The Demise of Ratners

Ratners was Britain's biggest retail jeweller operating a chain of high street stores selling inexpensive jewellery and gifts. Popular with young people and the less affluent, Ratners made its owner, Gerald Ratner, a lot of money. On 23rd April 1991, in a speech to The Institute of Directors, in London, Gerald Ratner discussed some of his products with an audience of UK business leaders and opinion formers telling them that an imitation book, with curled up corners was in the worst possible taste, 'but we sold a quarter of a million last year', he added, 'we also do cut glass sherry decanters, complete with six glasses on a silver plated tray all for £4.95. People say how can you sell this for such a low price? I say because it is total crap'. The quote was widely reported in the press and not surprisingly by June of that year the Daily Telegraph reported that the share price had dropped by 35p, (nearly 20%) and sales had also declined by 5%. The Group denied that the remark created a downturn in trading, but city analysts were more skeptical; Nick Hawkins of Kleinwort Benson, said 'there is no doubt that the comments would have affected the sales of some products, especially engagement rings'. Why should customers buy from someone who insulted them? Now renamed as Signet Group plc, the company is still operating. Whether Gerald Ratner's management philosophy really was to take the customer's money and sell them crap is doubtful, but that's exactly what many inferred following his comment. When working with customers, perceptions can be greater than realities. Gerald Ratner had inadvertently positioned his company as a vendor of inferior products.

Some philosophies have been well documented such as Kaizen, Empowerment and TQM, each of which is briefly discussed below together with why they are classified as assets.

Kaizen

Kaizen means continuous improvement. It is the name given to the Japanese management philosophy which calls for ongoing improvement involving everyone, including management and workers. In his book on *kaizen*, Masaaki Imai states that Japanese companies have developed a process-oriented way of thinking and develop strategies that ensure continuous improvement involving people at all levels of the organizational hierarchy. The message of *kaizen* is that there is not a day that should go by without some kind of improvement being made somewhere in the company. This is not a common management philosophy for Western companies, whose employees do not relish constant change, preferring to maintain the status quo. Western employees like to 'know where they are', and criticize management who keep the company in a constant state of change. Companies whose management philosophy calls for positive participation of all employees, have an asset that competitors cannot match overnight.

┌─ IC Concept#12 ───

Match Management Philosophy to Market Needs

└──

Empowerment

We have already stated that third millennium companies are likely to have a corporate culture which is moving from assertive to participative. If the company culture is participative employees have to have the responsibility, authority and be held accountable for their actions. They need to be empowered. A common ailment in some companies is the belief held by many employees that it is someone else's responsibility to ensure that the company is profitable, to keep spending under control and so on. The empowerment philosophy creates a state of mind within the work-force which calls on them to take power to change the work practices of the company for the better. Empowered individuals take the initiative. For some of us this is counter cultural, as we are brought up to do as we are told, not to take liberties and ensure we behave as we are expected to by our elders – growing up can be tough!

Empowerment is a two way process – managers can't just tell employees they are empowered and expect things to change. The onus is on individuals to take power. It's better to ask for forgiveness than permission. An empowered work-force is a great asset and it means that there are people in all levels of the company questioning processes and decisions and making things happen where there would previously have been inactivity.

Total Quality Management (TQM)

TQM and effective leadership is a management philosophy aimed at eliminating weaknesses which are perceived as 'the old ways'. Such weaknesses include:

- Doing what they have always done
- Not understanding or ignoring competitive pricing
- Compartmentalization
- Trying to control people through systems
- Confusing quality with grade

TQM aims to focus on quality at all stages of development and production of products and services, including the supplier chain. Like empowerment, the advantage of TQM is the number of employees concerned with the company's products and services throughout all aspects of the company. Focus on this aspect of the business by every employee is a significant asset.

Management Philosophy Audit Questions

- What is the management philosophy in your company?
- How is that philosophy communicated to others working in your company?
- Should this philosophy be communicated to others outside the company, such as customers and suppliers?
- Is the management philosophy in your company in tune with the achievement of corporate goals?
- Does the management philosophy need an overhaul?
- Is the management philosophy an asset or a liability?

IC Concept#13

Make Corporate Culture an Asset

CORPORATE CULTURE

Corporate culture can best be described as 'the way we do things around here'. It comprises values, heroes, rites and rituals that are recognized and shared by the work-force. It keeps the company safe from reacting to every market or management whim. A strong corporate culture which reflects a well considered management philosophy is a great asset. Corporate culture is created from the top of the company and typically reflects the values of the founders of the company. There are several types of cultures each determining the way individuals work and play together: macho, work-hard/play-hard, high-risk/high-reward, family-based, process-based, hero-based, team-based and so on. Clients in work-shops also described their cultures as 'entrepreneurial and excellent', 'honest and dependable' and so on. In large organizations employees don't perceive that their department has the same culture as the others. This is not surprising and different leaders will impose their values on group cultures.

Corporate Culture – Asset or Liability?

Corporate culture is an asset when the culture of the company reinforces achievement of corporate goals and reflects the management philosophy. It is a liability when there is a mismatch between culture, goals and management philosophy. For example, a specialist computer company with a process based culture is being whipped by the competition. A change is needed, so the investors bring in a new CEO. He decides to bring out a new machine in miracle time to rejuvenate the old product line. The company is under-resourced in R&D and cash flow is in bad shape. The CEO, who is a strong macho type, tells the sales force to preannounce the machine to the customers. The technical team responsible for the design of the new machine and the software to drive it, think the CEO is a jerk who doesn't understand the team process of bringing a new machine to market – which he doesn't. So he only deals with certain individuals in the company and beats up on anyone who points out potential problems or complains. The entire work-force is demoralized, there is is general feeling of doom and some employees leave. Under severe pressure to bring the product to market, after 6pm the R&D department is like the Marie Celeste. Everyone has gone home. They really don't care if the product makes it or not as they think the CEO may just fire them on a whim anyhow. The machine is completed, but it's late. The CEO orders it to be installed in customer sites before it's been properly tested and of course it fails. The company eventually goes into receivership.

This was a nasty situation for any CEO to fix, but the investors chose the wrong guy for the job. Such a difficult situation required a team builder who could inspire the work-force – someone who could get everyone to buy in to the process and work hard to get a quality product finished. Mismatch of management philosophy, corporate culture and new leadership style.

Corporate Culture Audit Questions
- What is the corporate culture of your company or department?
- Is the culture conducive to achieving corporate goals?
- Who are the heroes in your company?
- Why are these people heroes?

IC Concept#14

Collaborate for Greater Achievements

CORPORATE CULTURES AND COLLABORATION

There is a trend in industry for companies to come together to solve a problem or make a new product. This trend reflects the inability of today's companies to solve large problems and also an interest in extending the barriers of the company to include the supply chain. Companies in the third millennium will need to be able to collaborate in order to operate and pursue business. That ability is an asset. Whether or not two organizations can successfully work together is largely an issue of corporate culture – just wanting to work together is not enough. In their workshops on collaboration, The Technology Broker audited over 80 completed collaborations with workshop attendees who had been responsible for running business collaborations. The greatest reason for failure of collaborations was a mismatch of corporate cultures. In some cases corporate cultures are just too different for two companies to work together, but it's possible to get an initial feeling of differences by undertaking an audit with a potential collaborator before embarking on the collaboration.

Where the two responses to the questions are the same it presents no problem, where they are different the issue should be discussed.

Corporate Culture for Collaboration Audit

Part I – Management Style and Practice

	Partner 1	Partner 2
1. What is the major goal of this collaboration?		
Making Money	_____	_____
Technical Developments	_____	_____
Status	_____	_____
Developing Relationships	_____	_____
Industry Recognition	_____	_____
Other (specify)	_____	_____
2. How important is the success of the project?		
Vital	_____	_____
Very Important	_____	_____
Fairly Important	_____	_____
Not Very Important	_____	_____
Unimportant	_____	_____
Other (specify)	_____	_____
3. What motivates employees?		
Money	_____	_____
Status	_____	_____
Achieving the Goal	_____	_____
Industry Recognition	_____	_____
Other (specify)	_____	_____
4. How does the company share their equity?		
It Doesn't	_____	_____
Among all Employees	_____	_____
Only Among Senior Managers	_____	_____
Other (specify)	_____	_____

5. How does the company treat their customers?
   - Respectfully   _____   _____
   - Service Oriented   _____   _____
   - Obligingly   _____   _____
   - Distantly   _____   _____
   - As a Nuisance   _____   _____
   - As God   _____   _____
   - Other (specify)   _____   _____

6. How is success measured?
   - Job Done   _____   _____
   - Financially   _____   _____
   - Goals Achieved   _____   _____
   - Turnover   _____   _____
   - Profit Contribution   _____   _____
   - Other (specify)   _____   _____

7. How does the company get things done?
   - By Individuals   _____   _____
   - By Small Groups   _____   _____
   - By Large Groups   _____   _____
   - Teams   _____   _____
   - Quickly   _____   _____
   - Slowly   _____   _____
   - Other (specify)   _____   _____

8. How is the corporate hierarchy organized?
   - On Performance   _____   _____
   - Dead Men's Shoes   _____   _____
   - By Time Served   _____   _____
   - Other (specify)   _____   _____

9. How is success rewarded?
   - Private Recognition   _____   _____
   - Employee of the Month (or similar)   _____   _____
   - It Isn't   _____   _____
   - It Is Just Expected   _____   _____
   - Other (specify)   _____   _____

10. How does the company present
    itself to the outside world?
    The Best   _____   _____
    Professional   _____   _____
    High Quality   _____   _____
    Well Organized   _____   _____
    Cheap/Shoddy   _____   _____
    Other (specify)   _____   _____

11. How does the company
    treat their employees?
    As Individuals   _____   _____
    As Drones   _____   _____
    As a Resource   _____   _____
    As a Work-force   _____   _____
    Other (specify)   _____   _____

12. How does the company
    behave when things are bad?
    Fires People   _____   _____
    Tries Harder   _____   _____
    No Difference   _____   _____
    Other (specify)   _____   _____

13. How does the company
    behave when things are good?
    Spends Money   _____   _____
    Rewards Everyone   _____   _____
    Rewards Individuals   _____   _____
    Expands Business   _____   _____
    Other (specify)   _____   _____

14. How do people communicate
    at work?
    Memo   _____   _____
    Informal Meeting   _____   _____
    Formal Meeting as Needed   _____   _____
    Regular Meeting   _____   _____
    Other (specify)

15. How does the company
    view staff development?
    Important for All   _____   _____
    Important for Some   _____   _____
    Not Important   _____   _____
    Other (specify)   _____   _____

16. What kind of company
    cars do people have?
    They Don't   _____   _____
    Small   _____   _____
    Large   _____   _____
    Practical   _____   _____
    Flashy   _____   _____
    Basic   _____   _____
    Other (specify)   _____   _____

Part II – The People

	Partner 1	Partner 2
1. What kind of clothes do the people wear?		
Formal	_____	_____
Casual	_____	_____
Trendy	_____	_____
Classic	_____	_____
Business Suits	_____	_____
Trousers for Women	_____	_____
Other (specify)	_____	_____
2. What kind of jokes do they tell?		
Childish	_____	_____
Rude	_____	_____
Silly	_____	_____
Racist/Sexist	_____	_____
Other (specify)	_____	_____
3. How do people relate to their bosses?		
Formally	_____	_____
Friendly	_____	_____

Informally   ————   ————

Frequently   ————   ————

Rarely   ————   ————

Other (specify)   ————   ————

4. How do people relate to their peers?
   Formally   ————   ————
   Friendly   ————   ————
   Informally   ————   ————
   Frequently   ————   ————
   Rarely   ————   ————
   Other (specify)   ————   ————

5. How are people hired and fired?
   Quickly   ————   ————
   Slowly   ————   ————
   Long Interview   ————   ————
   Internally   ————   ————
   On Recommendation   ————   ————
   Other (specify)   ————   ————

6. How are people rewarded for
   doing a good job?
   Verbally   ————   ————
   Promotion   ————   ————
   Financially   ————   ————
   Extra Responsibility   ————   ————
   Other (specify)   ————   ————

7. What kind of guy makes a
   good employee?
   Young   ————   ————
   Mature   ————   ————
   Bright   ————   ————
   Has New Ideas   ————   ————
   Follows Company Lines   ————   ————
   A Loner   ————   ————
   Sense of Humour   ————   ————
   People Orientated   ————   ————
   Results Orientated   ————   ————
   Others (specify)   ————   ————

8. What do people think
   of collaborative ventures?
   Good Opportunity _____ _____
   Exciting _____ _____
   Hard Work _____ _____
   Nervous _____ _____
   Wary _____ _____
   Other (specify) _____ _____
   Why? _____ _____

9. What hours do people work?
   Long _____ _____
   Regular _____ _____
   Early Mornings _____ _____
   Late Nights _____ _____
   Weekends _____ _____
   Flexitime _____ _____
   Other (specify) _____ _____

10. How long do people stay with
    the company?
    Less than 1 Year _____ _____
    One to Five Years _____ _____
    Five to Ten Years _____ _____
    Over Ten Years _____ _____
    Other (specify) _____ _____

11. How long do people stay in the
    same job?
    Less than one year _____ _____
    One to Five Years _____ _____
    Five to Ten Years _____ _____
    Over Ten Years _____ _____
    Other (specify)

12. Do employees 'play' together
    Regularly _____ _____
    Often _____ _____
    Rarely _____ _____
    Never _____ _____
    In Small Groups _____ _____

In Large Groups	_____	_____
Other (specify)	_____	_____

13. Is the working environment?

Modern	_____	_____
Traditional	_____	_____
Pleasant	_____	_____
Dull	_____	_____
In Need of Decorating	_____	_____
Well Decorated	_____	_____
Other (specify)	_____	_____

14. Are there separate facilities for managers?

Toilets	_____	_____
Canteen	_____	_____
Car Parks	_____	_____
Other (specify)	_____	_____

15. Is the language used?

Formal	_____	_____
Informal	_____	_____
Friendly	_____	_____
Respectful	_____	_____
Peppered with Swearing	_____	_____
Other (specify)	_____	_____

Once both columns are complete, observe where the answers in the two columns differ greatly from each other. These points should be considered to see if they might lead to significant issues for the management team. Identify the major points of difference between the two organizations and plan accordingly.

Processes Which Implement Management Philosophy

Having a healthy corporate culture and a management philosophy which are in tune is not enough. Without management processes that implement philosophy, employees are discouraged and feel that management philosophy is all hype, and that nothing ever really changes. So it's essential to put mechanisms in place to turn philosophy into practice and ensure the people are in place to implement best practice. At the top of a company there's typically a leader or entrepreneur of some type, but these aren't typically the right people to implement management processes – the managers are. The types of processes that managers will implement are policies, quality control processes, a large variety of people related processes, *kaizen* practices such as staff suggestion boxes and procedures to evaluate their content and be a catalyst for change. Feedback mechanisms for all levels of management are required so that the management philosophy does not become out of tune with the needs of the market.

How to Listen to Followers

We have talked about leaders, entrepreneurs and managers, but in reality they represent the minority of the work-force, as most are followers and without them nothing would ever get done. Empowering followers can be tricky. Over the past three decades organizations have played a parent role with employees and in particular with followers, providing jobs, canteens, cars and for some even a reason for getting out of bed each morning. Now we are asking them to question, comment, suggest and participate. It's a complete role reversal and followers need to be motivated and rewarded for their participation in a process of continual improvement. At one conference, a very large US manufacturing company with facilities all over Asia was promoting the success of their suggestion box scheme. They quoted one female employee who had consistently made over 400 suggestions per annum for improvements to various factory activities, over 80% of which were implemented. When asked about the reward mechanism for such an observant and creative employee, several delegates were less than impressed to hear of a meal voucher scheme and wondered whether she'd really appreciate over 300 meal vouchers a year and why they didn't promote the employee to manager of the factory!

Information Technology Systems

IT systems provide the means to implement many management processes. Where they perform that function efficiently they become a corporate asset. Typically, computer equipment is considered as a tangible asset and appears on the balance sheet with other tangible assets. The cost of computer equipment and software has plummeted since the advent of systems standards, such as MS-DOS, UNIX and Microsoft Windows, but it's not the cost of buying the hardware we're talking about, it's the way IT solutions are used within the organization and their impact on efficiency, customer care, employee satisfaction and so on. The intangible benefits.

Information Technology Systems Audit Questions
- List the IT systems in your company.
- List who uses each system and why.
- List the number of reports generated by IT systems.
- List who needs and reads each report.
- What is the ratio of employee to PCs in your company?
- Is that ratio optimal?
- Is your company a company which is divided by IT systems or integrated by them?

Customer Databases and Customer Tracking

If an organization chooses a management philosophy which requires the organization to be customer driven, then an infrastructure needs to be put in place which enables that to happen. Most organizations keep customer databases but what do they use them for? The amount of information it is possible to keep on computer is limitless, as it's not only the information on the company, the account and its purchase history, but also information on the individuals who make purchase decisions, their favourite restaurants, the birthdays of family members, golf handicap and so on. After all, people buy from people. For the efficient organization, representation and maintenance of such information is an asset. To increase the value of this asset the information must be accurate. Query systems need to be designed and built which enable both sales staff, planners and whoever to access the data in a meaningful fashion. Such systems contribute towards keeping the 'evangelist' for life and ensuring repeat business, both valuable market assets.

Database Audit Questions

- How many databases are there in your company?
- What are they used for?
- How accurate are they?
- How are they maintained?
- Are they able to be queried to satisfy the user need?
- Would sharing them be valuable to others in the company?

NETWORKING SYSTEMS

Solitary computers are no longer an asset, but their ability to network with others, gaining access to customers, suppliers, other R&D organizations, databases and so on is essential for third millennium companies. Communications infrastructures can be implemented using electronic mail, or software such as Lotus Notes. Such systems are not only faster than paper, they remove our reliance on it. Organizations who subscribe to the Internet can communicate at low cost anywhere on the planet with someone who has access to a computer. It's difficult to estimate exactly how many people are currently using Internet because of shared addresses, computers and so on – but the British magazine *.net* estimates that in February 1996 there were 33.7 million users compared with 26.2 million in May 1995. The Internet is predicted by some to be having the same impact as the telephone has had.

The World Wide Web

The World Wide Web (WWW) gives its users the ability to communicate with each other not just by text, but also with graphics, sound animation and colour. Use of the WWW can be an asset as organizations can set up Web pages, which act as signposts to others who may wish to know more about the company's products and services, its research or its people. The WWW can be an extension of corporate marketing, public relations and even the sales channel. Goods can be offered for sale, payment accepted and where the goods are digital they can even be delivered in what has become known as the market space.

Organizations are gearing up to this new communications medium, even governments. In its 1995 Awards for Excellence the UK based magazine *Computing* awarded the CCTA – the government's IT advisory body – the Gold Award for Internet User of the Year. The award, targeted at organizations using Internet to enhance their performance, was won by CCTA for its Government Information Service, which gives the public access to 80 public sector organizations, 15 major government departments and 50 government agencies. Using the Web as a communications mechanism can be developed into an infrastructure asset if careful consideration is given to the establishment of a Web service which reflects management philosophy. Options are varied, an information service, a feedback mechanism for customers, a marketing mechanism or even a distribution mechanism.

Teleworking

The work day for many of us is changing. We can communicate with our colleagues and customers via e-mail, Internet, the Web and by phone. We don't need secretaries because most of us can use a personal computer for correspondence, design and planning. Using groupware solutions which co-ordinate team effort we can even design and produce products. If we want to see our colleagues we can use video conferencing or video phones. The need to travel is greatly reduced. Even the need to go to an office. Teleworkers, or workers who work remotely from their office, enable the organization to cut down the cost of operating expensive office buildings. So infrastructure which enables teleworkers to be more productive and satisfied employees is an asset. Technology which enables teleworking means communities can work from home whereas previously they could not cope with the rigours of working nine to five. Examples include parents, the disabled and those who are geographically remote who would otherwise have long journeys to work.

Networking Audit Questions

- What use is made of e-mail, Internet and the WWW in your company?
- Is the corporate image maintained when these systems are used?
- How will your company use networking over the next five years?
- Does your company have any teleworkers?

- Is it appropriate for your company to have teleworkers?
- How can a teleworking community be organized to make your company more efficient, and satisfy needs of the employees?

┌─ IC Concept#15 ─────────────────────────────────────

IT Infrastructure is Corporate Backbone

The Changing Role of the IT Manager

Historically, the person who was in charge of computer systems was the IT manager. Positioned as the person who ran the big mainframe computers in air-conditioned rooms, many would say that they are an anachronism. Today lots of people in the organization are computer buffs. They have computers at home and at the office. They read *PC Week*, *Byte* and *MacWorld*. They don't need advice from the mainframe guys to buy a piece of software. Maybe not. But weaving many PCs together – in the office and employees' homes – with mainframes and legacy systems to create an IT infrastructure is an expert function. Security is a major concern. If teleworkers are going to be accessing the organization's databases remotely, careful consideration must be given to the protection of these valuable assets. IT managers have many of the skills to tackle this task, but their role in the company needs to be reinvented, just as the role of human resource managers needs to be reinvented to respond to the new shape of the enterprise. The IT manager is really the infrastructure guy, whose job it should be to work with vertical business groups to ensure that they can view the organization and its resources from whatever aspect they need and that they have the optimal infrastructure to support their work processes.

IT Manager Audit Questions

- What role does the IT manager have in developing and implementing corporate strategy?
- What mechanisms does your company use to predict a requirement for IT infrastructure over a three to five year period?
- What mechanisms does your IT manager use to keep up to date on evolving technology which could be used by your company?

- Where is your company on the adoption of innovation curve below?

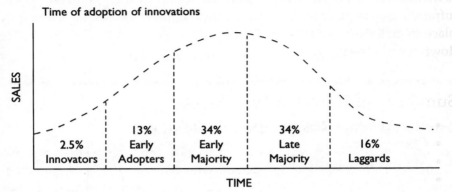

Figure 6.1 The innovation curve

- Is this position appropriate to achieve corporate goals?

FINANCIAL RELATIONS

Financial relations are an asset because when the company wants room to manoeuvre, favourable relations with investors, banks and so on provide that space. Investor relations is a mechanism used by most large companies who seek to keep industry analysts secure in the belief that changes in strategy are beneficial to the overall value of stock. Companies who alienate the financial community can see the consequences in a drop in stock value. For small companies it pays to romance the banks and business angels to whom they may turn for all forms of assistance. Individuals who establish a healthy infrastructure with the financial community are developing an asset which should remain after they have left the company.

Do Infrastructure Assets Support Achievement of Corporate Goals?

Finally, it's important to examine whether or not the organization has the appropriate infrastructure assets in place to achieve its corporate goals. This is a strategic question. So the new role of the IT manager is really about strategy not just implementation. It's also a job which can never be finished, as the infrastructure must bend with the organization to respond to market needs. No company can rest on its laurels and say that it has the infrastructure in place to achieve corporate goals. If the infrastructure is in place to achieve this year's goals, better be ready to modify it or tear it down for next year.

Summary of Infrastructure Assets

- Management philosophy
- Corporate culture
- Management processes
- Information technology systems
- Networking systems
- Financial relations

7

Planning an Intellectual Capital Audit

It was a long time before anyone spoke. Out of the corner of his eye Phouchg could see the sea of tense expectant faces down in the square outside.

'We're going to get lynched aren't we?' he whispered.

'It was a tough assignment,' said Deep Thought mildly.

'Forty-two!' yelled Loonquawl. 'Is that all you've got to show for seven and a half million years' work?'

'I checked it very thoroughly,' said the computer, 'and that quite definitely is the answer. I think the problem, to be quite honest with you, is that you've never actually known what the question is.'

The Hitchhikers Guide to the Galaxy, Douglas Adams

THE GENERIC INTELLECTUAL CAPITAL AUDIT

In a generic intellectual capital audit we would look at all the intangible assets in the company and document their existence, current state and maybe their value. For employees we would document their education, put each one through a set of psychometric and personality tests to discover the potential of every employee. We would discover who could think critically, sell products and services, provide dexterity skills and work in teams. The attributes of the individual are far more numerous than there are tests to identify their richness. It would also be necessary to look at all intellectual property rights, all trade marks and all know-how. The end result would be an immense amount of knowledge about intangible assets. This would enable us to determine how many people had tertiary education, how many people had been with the company for more than ten years, how many customers we had, how many patents we had and what it cost to maintain them. In short, it would help us to generate statistics which may or may not be useful information. The problem with a generic audit is that because we are dealing with intangibles, notably humans, the process would never ever conclude. It is therefore important to have a goal in mind before an audit is planned.

IC Concept#16

Identify Goals, Audit Intangibles, Assess Strength

Why Undertake an Intellectual Capital Audit?

Knowledge of intellectual capital is a rich source of information about the organization and is of particular value in the following scenarios:

- Validating the organization's ability to achieve its goals.
- Planning research and development.
- Providing background information for re-engineering programmes.
- Providing focus for organizational education and training programmes.
- Assessing the value of the enterprise.
- Expanding an organizational memory.

Validating the Organization's Ability to Achieve its Goals

Strategic planning and goal setting are ways companies seek to plan their future. However, from time to time management plans are not able to be fulfilled, not because the plan is faulty, but because the resource is not in place to make the plan succeed. It is easy to tell if a plan will fail due to lack of tangible assets – not enough cash, not the right machinery and so on – but determining if the intangible assets are in place is currently difficult for the strategist to determine. Are the people we employ today the right ones to make us successful in the next century? Do we have the business processes in place which will support the goals we have set? Intellectual capital audits will provide knowledge about such issues and help identify the gaps which must be filled if the strategy is to be successful.

Planning Research and Development

Why organizations undertake R&D is not always clear. The simple answer is to generate new products and services for the future, but the trade off between research to generate know-how and research to develop patents or new designs is unclear. Many organizations who keep a patent portfolio do so as a defence mechanism, as armour against some unseen threat. However, patents are expensive to maintain and the main benefit of the R&D may not be the patent, but the know-how generated during the project. If know-how reflects competitive advantage, then organizations need to understand the nature of know-how in their possession and how to protect and increase it to competitive advantage. An intellectual capital audit of the R&D function will provide the knowledge needed with which to evaluate and design R&D programmes.

Providing Background Information for Re-engineering Programmes

When organizations decide to downsize or re-engineer, decisions must be made concerning human assets. Who stays? Who is made redundant? What jobs or functions will be merged in the new organization? These decisions are often made in a vacuum, as human assets are evaluated in an ad-hoc fashion. An intellectual capital audit will provide valuable knowledge for executives who are planning to re-engineer or downsize, ensuring that neither of these processes inadvertently divests the organization of valuable capability and know-how.

Providing Focus for Organizational Education and Training Programmes

It is currently fashionable for companies to refer to themselves as 'learning organizations'. In addition, organizations are ranked on how much training they provide for their employees. Whether that training is germane in enabling the organization to meet its goals is often not considered. Training and education are a means of improving know-how and the value of human-centred assets. It should be considered in that light and knowledge resulting from an intellectual capital audit will help in planning education and training programmes which are of benefit both to the individual and the organization.

Assessing the Value of the Enterprise

When valuing an enterprise businessmen look to the book value. In many organizations the book value is low, but their actual value may be high. Examples include software companies where the know-how to build software is the greatest asset the organization possesses. Alternatively, the organization may be young and have few tangible assets, yet its people have track records in their own right which should be counted as intangible assets. An intellectual capital audit provides in-depth knowledge of the intangible assets of the organization, which can be used to support the tangibles, giving analysts and financiers an information-rich perspective of the organization.

Expanding an Organizational Memory

Organizations spend huge sums of money paying for employees to reinvent the wheel. Skills possessed by individuals remain a mystery to others who have to develop them in order to do their job. The IC knowledge base, which will contain information on 'who has what skills', can be built as a result of an intellectual capital audit and forms the basis for an 'organizational memory'. It also provides the potential to boost the 20% utilization figure cited by The Gottilieb Duttweiler Institute. Organizations of the future will have staff whose job it is to maintain the organizational memory which will become a valuable intangible asset in its own right.

'You Cannot Step Twice Into the Same River...' Heraclitus

One of the nice things about working with companies is that they are always trying to go somewhere. Even if that 'somewhere' is to stay where they are. Nothing ever really stands still. Time and the market are constantly changing. Therefore they have to exist in a state of transition. This state of transition means that there is a notion of movement, of where they want to go – a goal. Companies are in a state of transition whether they want to be or not. They are on a journey through an environment which is in constant change – the market, technology, competitors, everything. The role of the CEO is to guide the company through the never-ending state of transition, using resources in the optimal fashion. For the IC auditor this is a convenient way to view the world as it provides them with the two essential components which are required to analyse intellectual capital – a goal and a current state.

The term 'audit' is normally used in conjunction with accounting, its role being to verify that the accounts represent a true and fair view of the company's financial situation. When looking at intellectual capital, the term 'audit' is used in a wider context – to monitor, watch and oversee the intellectual capital of a company. Individuals undertaking audits of accounts have guidelines to help in the valuation of certain assets. Land or office space is valued for a geographical area, vehicles have a book value depending on the year they were built, computers are valued on their age, together with an acceptable rate of depreciation. Accounting audits do not concern themselves with whether or not the fleet of vehicles is the right fleet for the job, or whether a patent owned by the company is generating its optimal revenue. However, the existence of an employee whose knowledge and skills are underutilized is of great concern to the intellectual capital auditor. In auditing intellectual capital, we are concerned with achieving the optimal state for intangible assets. This of course begs the question, 'How do you know when assets are being optimally used?' There are two ways to respond to this question. The first is to treat the question as a philosophical one, and dedicate a great deal of time to its answer, which isn't very practical. The alternative is to define a hypothetical state, 'assets are optimally used', in the context of the goals of the organization. We refer to this state as high-values.

Intangible assets can make the difference between a company operating efficiently or not. Consider some of the following problems and how a company might go about achieving the transition:

- A company wants to change its business from computer manufacturer to systems integrator. In order to achieve the transition they decide to empower their staff, creating a middle management of entrepreneurial types who can manage business collaborations – typical to the business of systems integrators. The top management thinks it has empowered its staff, but the required change in staff behaviour has not happened. How do you determine what the problem is?

- A company has been selling services for five years. Ten percent of their revenues comes from repeat business. They would like to increase that number to thirty percent to help cut the cost of sales. How do they achieve that goal?

- A very large manufacturing company with a wide range of electrical and white goods products runs four research laboratories. Between them they register several hundred patents each year. One of the labs decided to look at the revenue directly generated by its patents and discovered they only generated $250,000 and needed twice that to maintain them. What should they do?

Each of the above examples requires the examination of the company's intellectual capital to discover how it is being used and whether or not it's able to contribute to a corporate transition.

In general, IC audits are used to see if available resources are in place to make a transition and to identify resources which need to be acquired to 'fill the holes'. As there will always be a goal, it's possible to visualize an optimal asset set, that is, the best possible resources – regardless of whether or not the company knows it has those assets. Examples of an optimal asset set could be:

Trade mark and repeat business

Trade mark is 100% recognition and repeat business is 100% customer base. This means that every person who saw the trade mark would recognize it and every customer who ever bought would buy again. The fact that this state may be unachievable for any company doesn't matter because it provides a focus and a means of measuring intellectual capital against a goal.

STEPS IN UNDERTAKING AN IC AUDIT

There are hundreds of ways in which we can think of intangible assets. For example, we could measure the number of employees who had graduate education, or the number of patents filed, but what would that actually tell us? Without an identified transition or goal, not a lot. The following steps describe a top level view of an intellectual capital audit.

1 Identify the transition, goals, domain and constraints
2 Determine optimal aspect set
3 Assign high values to aspects
4 Choose audit method
5 Audit aspect
6 Document asset value in IC Knowledge Base

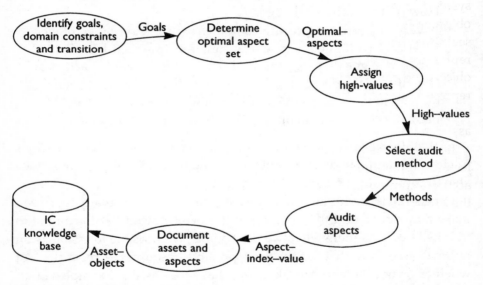

Figure 7.1 The intellectual capital audit process

Each of these six steps will be looked at in detail in Chapter 8.

A Note on Process Diagrams

Process diagrams are useful to help identify the steps which need to be followed in order to achieve a task. They are driven by data and are sometimes also called data-flow diagrams. It's important to note that each bubble represents a process, and the arrows which emerge out of a bubble drive the process in the next bubble. Every arrow coming out of a bubble must be labelled. If you find it difficult to label the arrow coming out differently from the one which went in then it's probably a non-process and it should be omitted. There is also no control flow. This means that we can focus on what to do at a high level of abstraction.

The IC audit process assumes a transition process which most IC audits are undertaken to respond to. The terminology of the audit, together with the process is explained below.

Documenting the Audit

The audit will generate a vast amount of information and knowledge which needs to be documented and stored, ultimately in a computer system. In preparation for that activity we are using a notation called object orientation. Object orientation is an organizational technique which seeks to model the way we view the world. It lends itself very well to the representation of intellectual capital as it works equally well with simple objects and complex concepts such as the representation of knowledge. By representing the findings of the audit with this notation we are automatically defining the nature of the computer system which will eventually assist in the management of intellectual capital.

In order to be explicit when we communicate the findings of an intellectual capital audit, there is an accepted terminology we use which aids accurate communication. There are a few concepts which are pertinent to the use of the notation:

- Concepts or object types
- Objects
- Associations and mappings
- Relationship types
- Subtypes
- States

Concepts or object types

A concept is an idea or notion that we can apply to the things or objects in our awareness. Object types can be both tangible such as a person or intangible such as quality. They can represent events, such as product launch, and roles, such as manager. As humans we apply concepts to objects. So we can apply the concept of success to an object such as a business or a person. Our reality is based on applying conceptual tests to objects. Concepts are shared between groups of people and consensus becomes the norm. So if a group of people in the same company applied the same concept, 'best meeting of the week' to the object 'Friday beer bust' then we could deduce that cultural element of the company was strong.

Figure 7.2 Concepts – 'best meeting of the week'

Objects

An object is anything to which a concept applies. It can be a sales quota, a backlog, a patent, anything. Objects can be grouped in to sets, such as the set of intellectual property asset objects, or the set of vehicles, or a set of employees. Objects can be members of more than one set, for example, the object Andrew is a member of the set male and the set Range Rover owners. Know-how is a member of the set intellectual property and human-centred asset.

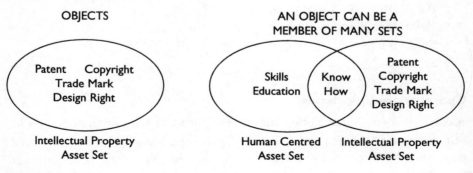

Figure 7.3 Objects

Associations and Mappings

Association provides a means to link objects of various types in a meaningful way. Figure 7.4 shows two sets of objects, a set of scientists and a set of patents. The set of patents has instances of patents A, B, C, D, E, F and G. The object set of scientists has instances Nick, David and Peter. The lines show the associations between the instances in the two sets: David and Peter are the inventors of patent G, Nick and Peter patents B and F and Nick patent A. There are no associations for patents C, D and E.

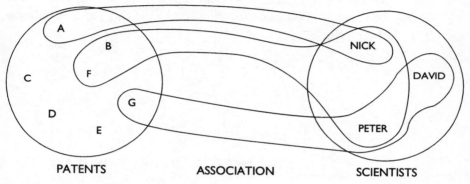

Figure 7.4 Associations

Mappings assign objects of one type to objects of another type. In Figure 7.5 we can see two sets – Departments and Managers. Each set has three objects. The arrows represent a mapping instance of 'manages'. Mappings usually have inverse mapping which means that they can represent all of the manage-related instances between the two.

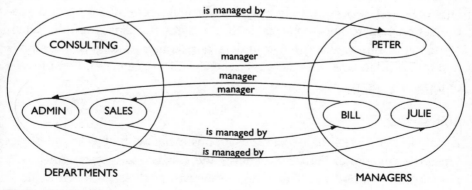

Figure 7.5 Mappings

Relationship Types

Relationships types are those which have tuples, pairs joined by a relationship like a man and wife. Sometimes there are more than two who make up a relationship, and in that case they are referred to as n-tuples. In Figure 7.6 we show two sets, Company X and Company Y. In Company X there are three objects Nick, Bill and Victoria; in Company Y there are four objects Julie, Peter, Edward and David. Julie, Bill and Nick have a relationship as they are involved in the same collaboration. Edward and Victoria are involved in a different collaboration. Relationships can have properties, for example, collaboration A could be ranked 9 and collaboration B could be ranked 10.

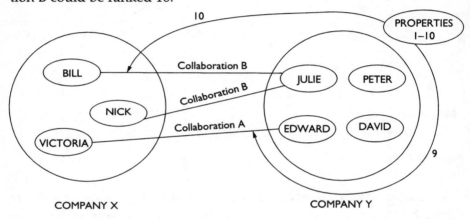

Figure 7.6 Relationships

Subtypes and Supertypes

Subtypes and supertypes are ways of showing generalization and specialization and to show objects within a hierarchy. For example, when considering representing the founders of a company, Figure 7.7 shows that all founders are stock holders, who are all managers and employees of the same company.

States

A state is a collection of associations an object has with objects and object types. For example, Figure 7.8 shows the state of an object which is a patent for a mousetrap. This simple diagram enables us to build up a picture of IC which is a rich way of communicating complex knowledge.

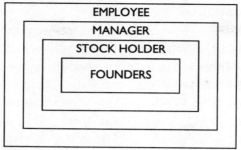

Figure 7.7 Subtypes and supertypes

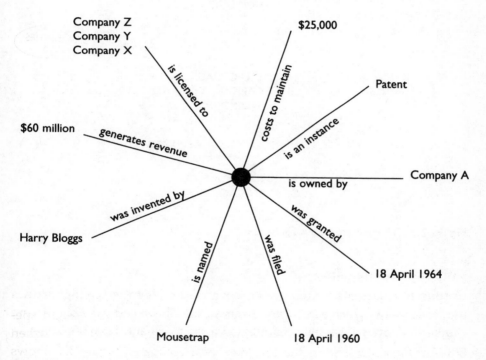

Figure 7.8 States

Putting the Intellectual Capital Audit Team Together

Finally the intellectual capital audit team needs to be pulled together. The skills needed may already be in the company, some may need to be imported from outside by using consultants. Six different types of skills are required in order to undertake an audit:

- Corporate strategists
- Finance experts
- Human resource experts
- Knowledge analysts
- Intellectual property experts
- Marketing experts

The role of each is discussed below.

Figure 7.9 The intellectual capital audit team

Corporate Strategists

Corporate strategists are required to set goals and help assign high values as measures by which assets can be measured. They need to be big picture thinkers, know where the organization aims to go and how it's going to get there.

Finance Experts

Finance experts are needed for the valuation process, but these individuals must also have a knowledge of legal aspects of assets, such as intellectual property, in order to be able to value them.

Human Resource Experts

Human resource experts are needed to give and evaluate occupational assessment tests. They are also required to help identify key skills required by the work-force in order for the organization to be able to achieve its goals.

Knowledge Analysts

Knowledge analysts are required to work with individuals in the organization to identify key knowledge assets. They will plan and perform the knowledge elicitation and analysis phase of the project, identifying different types of knowledge which are required in order to perform particular tasks.

Intellectual Property Experts

Intellectual property experts are required in order to assess the strength of patent and other forms of intellectual property rights protection. They do not need to be patent attorneys, but rather have an understanding of the business implications of ownership of a particular piece of intellectual property.

The intellectual capital audit team should be planned as a permanent fixture, its multidisciplinary nature enabling each team member to learn from the others over a period of time. Ultimately, the organization requires individuals who possess a mixture of skills, say marketing, intellectual property and strategic planning, or intellectual property, finance and corporate strategy, or human resources, knowledge analysis and strategic planning. Then the true intellectual capital professional is born.

IC Concept# 17

Auditing Intellectual Capital Needs Multidisciplinary Teams

Checklist for IC Audit Planning:

- Are the motives for the audit agreed and documented?
- Who will carry out the audit?
- Do the team have an agreed method of notation for documenting and communicating their findings?
- Who is the audience for the findings of the audit?
- Has the optimal state of assets been identified and agreed?

8

The Intellectual Capital Audit

The audit has been chosen, the reason for the audit has been explained by management, now it's time to start work. The process the team will follow is the same as in Figure 7.1 which is shown again here in Figure 8.1.

1 IDENTIFY THE TRANSITION, GOALS, DOMAIN AND CONSTRAINTS

The transition is the change in state which is required by the company. Examples of transitions are:

- I'd like the company to be as profitable next year as it was this year.
- I'd like us to reduce the cost of sales.
- The company should offer its services twenty-four hours a day.

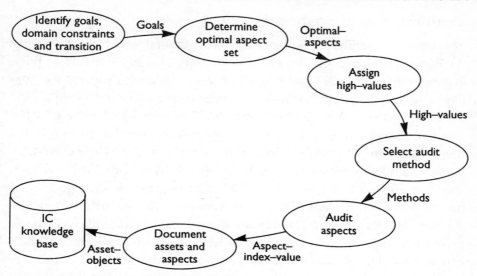

Figure 8.1 The intellectual capital audit process

Paradoxically, staying in the same place is still a transition, as even though the company is trying to stay in the same place, time and the market move on.

Goals

The goal is the goal of the audit. It should be as specific as possible. Whilst it may be interesting to undertake an intellectual capital audit to see what intangible assets the company has, the process will be very time consuming if it lacks focus. Once an initial management policy for intellectual capital has been identified the process can be ongoing, but in general it is wise to start with a very specific goal. Examples of goals include:

- To evaluate whether resources are able to achieve corporate goals.
- To prepare a company for flotation.
- To validate strategy and assets for investors.
- To prepare to design corporate learning services.
- To prepare for re-engineering.
- To assess a requirement to grow or acquire additional assets.

IC Concept#18

Measurement Identifies Assets

Domains and Constraints

The notion of undertaking an intellectual capital audit can be pretty daunting. That's because the initial perception of many is that it's a huge exercise which involves auditing all of the intellectual property, exhaustively interviewing and testing every employee, customer and supplier – it's never ending. An IC audit isn't an all or nothing exercise and the problem space must be pruned so that the problem is solvable. In fact, it's much better to focus on the important aspects of the business first, or those which for one reason or another aren't working properly. Having a specific issue to examine makes the IC audit much more manageable – it provides focus. Problem solving can best be managed by defining the problem and its domain. The domain defines the world within which the problem will be considered, together with the assets, aspects and their behaviours. The domain is bounded by constraints which limit the problem space. For example, the question to be answered could be:

How Can We Generate More Revenue?

There are millions of potential answers to that question, including close the company down and start over, which may not be acceptable to the CEO or the investors. The domain is identified with constraints by expanding the question to:

How can we generate more revenue within six months?

How can we generate more revenue from our intellectual property without hiring more staff? or

How can we generate more revenue from our existing customers?

— IC Concept#19 —

Know What Optimal Looks Like

---

2 DETERMINE OPTIMAL ASPECT SET

An aspect is one facet of an asset. Assets have multiple aspects. For example the market asset, customer base, has the following aspects.

It is only necessary to look at relevant aspects of an asset during the audit. If the purpose of the audit is to consider brand loyalty, the value and other aspects of the brand may not be relevant. It's a matter of 'divide

ASSET: CUSTOMER BASE	
ASPECTS	SIZE
	REPEAT BUSINESS
	CUSTOMER PROFILE
	BRAND LOYALTY

Figure 8.2 Aspects of the customer base

and conquer'. The combined aspects of assets we decide to examine in an audit is called a viewpoint.

3 ASSIGN HIGH VALUES TO ASPECTS

High values are assigned to aspects of an asset in order to provide focus for the audit. They are the optimal state the aspect could be in, for a particular company. Examples of high values of an aspect could be:

ASSET	ASPECT	HIGH VALUES
TRADE MARK	VALUE $	$10 MILLION
KNOW-HOW	DESIGNING MICROCHIPS	50 EMPLOYEES
REPEAT BUSINESS	% CUSTOMER BASE	100%

Figure 8.3 Examples of high values assigned to aspects of assets

4 CHOOSE AUDIT METHOD

Audit methods are those which enable the auditor to determine the current state of an aspect. There are many methods which map to particular aspects. Examples of methods roughly grouped by appropriate class are outlined in the table below:

IC Concept#20

Validate the Market – Measure Market Assets

Methods for Evaluating Market Assets

MARKET ASSETS	Customer Survey	Customer Interview	Analyse Sales	Analyse Cost of Sale	Market Research	Audit Agreements	Competitive Analysis	Determine ROI	Analyse Payments
Service Brands	✔	✔			✔		✔	✔	
Product Brands	✔	✔			✔		✔	✔	
Corporate Brands	✔	✔			✔		✔	✔	
Champions		✔			✔				
Customers		✔			✔				
Evangelists		✔			✔				
Customer Loyalty	✔	✔			✔		✔	✔	
Repeat Business	✔	✔	✔	✔	✔		✔	✔	
Company Name	✔	✔			✔			✔	
Backlog			✔		✔		✔	✔	✔
Distribution Channels	✔	✔	✔	✔	✔	✔	✔	✔	✔
Business Collaborations		✔	✔		✔	✔	✔	✔	✔
Franchise Agreements			✔	✔	✔	✔	✔	✔	✔
Licensing Agreements			✔	✔	✔	✔	✔	✔	✔
Favourable Contracts	✔	✔	✔	✔	✔	✔	✔	✔	

Figure 8.4 Methods for auditing market assets

Methods for auditing market assets include: customer survey, customer interviews, analysis of sales data, analysis of cost of sales, market research, audit of agreements, competitive analysis, evaluation of ROI, analysis of payments. Most of the methods will be well-known to the reader and although it sounds easy to dash off a questionnaire, or perform market research, all these methods will not yield useful knowledge about the state of an asset unless the IC auditor asks the right question and the method provides the answer. Simple, but the vast majority of projects we have seen can't do it. So once a campaign or questionnaire is designed it's essential to determine exactly what the questionnaire or survey will deliver, lots of information, to be sure, but lots of useful information?

Customer Survey

Surveying the customers is always a good idea for many reasons, if not only to keep in touch with the customers. One client, a CEO of an old family-owned dentistry supplies company was having a problem determining if the direct sales mechanism he was using was appropriate. He was dumbstruck when it was suggested he ask his bigger customers if the channel worked for them next time he met them, say over lunch.

'But I don't have lunch with the customers', he protested,

So we suggested he brought up the issue at the end of a meeting.

'I don't meet with them either', he said, 'I never have and neither did my father or grandfather before him'.

Our turn to be dumbstruck.

Customer surveys are appropriate to determine the strength of market assets when the questions are 'Why' type questions.

Why do customers buy our products, brands, services – giving information on positioning, brand strength, brand loyalty, the distribution mechanism, the positioning of the company, whether or not advertising is hitting the mark. Important factors include sample size, methods of selecting respondents and phraseology of questions – all of which are specialist skills.

Customer Interviews

Customer interviews are appropriate when a detailed profile of a customer is required. Customer interviews are typically more in-depth activities than surveys and are often recorded using audio or video equipment. Interviewers should have a predetermined set of questions identified that they require answers to, but that's not to say the questions will ever be asked directly. Free-flow interviews, where the interviewer gently leads the customer to talk about an issue, can give an enormous quantity of information. Again, focus can be an issue and gifted interviewers are always in control of the interview even though it may seem that they are just listening.

Opportunities to watch the customer are useful. We have already mentioned that we are living in an increasingly ageing society. One impact of this is that there is a huge percentage of older car drivers. The oldest car driver in the UK is a hundred and four years old – he drives himself to work every day! Yet cars are designed by and for young people. So, repeat business in this market sector is likely to be reliant on whether an aged driver can open the car door, get in and out of it, see through the wind-screen and use the steering wheel. Forget the CD and cassette player with tiny rubber controls – arthritic fingers have no use for them!

The biggest problem with using audio and video technique is unscrambling a huge quantity of audio or video material and analysing it. Product designers and technical staff should be exposed to this process as the result is usually a revelation for the technical person who rarely sees the customer.

Analysis of Sales Data

Analysis of sales data is useful in situations such as percentage of repeat business, buying patterns, determining backlog profiles, assessing the performance of the channel and whether or not agreements such as franchise and licensing agreements are effective. Analysis of sales data will answer 'What' questions, so they are frequently the predecessor of survey and interview techniques which answer 'Why' questions. It is always interesting to compare values for projected sales, channel capacity and the sales cycle. In every study we have ever undertaken there is a mismatch between these three, giving a false interpretation on channel performance.

When the Numbers Don't Add Up

A company achieved 50% of projected sales. The immediate reaction was that the channel wasn't working and indeed was a corporate liability not an asset. The marketing department had projected sales of 10% of the market, say 100 units, which they thought was modest. The product was a high value complex piece of computer equipment, which on average took nine months to sell from the first call to closing the sale. A sales-person could cope with twenty emerging sales at any one time, but had a close rate of 25%. Therefore, to close 100 sales, four hundred suspects needed to be identified and started on the process of moving through the sales cycle. If the sales rep could cope with twenty suspects at a time who took nine months to close, assuming he replenished suspects who dropped out of the sales process along the way, the company would need 4 or 5 sales reps to close 100 units. They had two, who were working day and night. There are two issues which need examination in this type of situation concerning the state of assets. The first is that the channel was in good shape, but needed expanding, providing it could be established that the other 5% market share was really there. The second is that the marketing department was in poor shape as it didn't understand the logistics associated with the sales process.

Analysis of Cost of Sales

Analysis of cost of sales is a good metric when looking at the value and efficiency of the distribution channel. Companies have different ways in which they choose to determine this metric. In recent years some companies have chosen unconventional methods to sell products, with great success. Dell Computers has built a valuable business selling computers using direct sales and telesales techniques, as do a number of software companies including Oracle and Gupta. It is interesting to ponder a reaction to the idea to sell computers and software over the phone had the suggestion been made in 1970.

Collaborative business arrangements such as licensing and franchising are always worth examining if cost of sales looks high. Clearly not all businesses generate suitable products, services and intellectual property for such arrangements, but if a distribution channel is a high value asset it's essential to keep it very healthy and prosperous for both the company and the sales-force. It costs a huge amount of money to put such a channel in place and wait out the honeymoon period whilst the sales staff settle in and establish a backlog. It can disappear almost overnight if not properly maintained and motivated.

Market Research

If there is one universal corporate function which is under-utilized and undervalued it's market research. It is rare that a company does too much market research. Market research is a fine indicator when looking at every aspect of market assets. Creative market research will identify 'flurries', that exciting time just before a trend emerges when a number of key indicators all say the same thing. Companies who are able to identify flurries have a rare market advantage.

Back to the Body Shop

A good example of a flurry which led to significant market assets in positioning, branding, distribution channel and packaging strategy was the Body Shop, founded by Anita Roddick in March 1976.

Overflowing with corporate idealism, The Body Shop leaned heavily on suppliers to adopt similar ethical and environmental standards to its own. Products were made of natural ingredients, which were easily renewable and not scarce or under threat. They insisted suppliers sign a mandate confirming that none of the ingredients had been tested on animals in the previous five years, either by themselves or by their suppliers.

'I was not in the least surprised by the upsurge of the Green movement in the Eighties,' said Roddick. 'What surprised me was how long it took for the media and politicians to cotton on to it'. The early policy of refilling bottles was developed out of necessity – they could not afford to buy enough. So the Body Shop started promoting recycling long before it became ecologically fashionable. The time was ripe for The Body Shop, its corporate position stood for what so many of its customers believed in and it arrived at exactly the right time. In her book *Anita Roddick – Body and Soul*, she doesn't claim to have done any market research, or been able to predict the green movement, so it might seem strange to use the example. Suffice it to say that in doing market research these would be exactly the flurries to look for!

Market Research as a Comfort Blanket

There are lots of professional market research companies from whom reports can be purchased which predict how markets grow. Such documents are usually expensive and many executives use them as comfort blankets. If the market research says so, then it must be OK. Generic market research reports are just that. They give the reader lots of information about the market, but not from the viewpoint of an individual company. Sadly, market research has a low calibre profile. Colleagues may consider it to be the bum job, but it's the most valuable role in the business of assessing market assets, too valuable to take the word of a third party. So if it's a comfort blanket you want, buy market research reports. If it's information about your market and customers – do your own.

Audit of Agreements

Audit of agreements is important to ensure that the original motivation for the agreement is still valid. Large collaborations sometimes take on a life and existence all of their own. Over the last five years we have audited over a hundred collaborative ventures and have discovered huge reluctance to closing down something which makes no sense. Apart from executive egos which will get bruised as a result, the lost opportunity cost of participating in a bad project can be the final straw in a recessive economy. Quarterly review of all collaborations is essential which should include review of agreements, market survey, competitive analysis, whatever is necessary to validate the existence of the arrangement.

Competitive Analysis

Like market research, competitive analysis is a weakness for many companies. Unlike market research, the use of an objective third party is a great idea for competitive analysis provided they think they won't be the messenger who gets shot. Exhaustive competitive analysis should be kept regularly up to date to support activity to strengthen all market assets. The list of assets on which to gather information is long, almost everything from the competitor's position, brand strength, products, services, distribution channel, everything they have. This information enables the company to rank itself against its competitors and provides a wealth of information for strategic planning to beat the competition.

Evaluation of ROI

Evaluation of ROI on all market aspects is a metric which should be checked fairly regularly in order to prioritize investment in all assets. The ROI calculation will have to be customized for every asset and company as the ROI may not be direct, or easy to calculate.

Analysis of Payments

An analysis of payments should give an indication of whether agreements are active and in force. Where the payment is a royalty, most agreements provide a mechanism to audit the books of the licensor in order to determine that his payments are in accordance with the agreement. There is huge reluctance in industry to invoke this clause. In 1993 The Technology Broker published its first report on the financial control of licensing agreements. The report summarized the findings of a survey of fifty-five organizations involved in technology transfer and licensing. It excluded anyone dealing with entertainment copyright licensing, such as record companies. The businesses and organizations included private limited companies, university technology transfer business units and research charities from a broad base of industrial sectors in all geographical areas of the UK. Industry sectors included biotechnology, pharmaceuticals, IT, electronics and engineering. Of those who did license technology, a total of 78% (39) confirmed that their agreements included audit clauses, giving the right to inspection of books by an independent auditor, 22% (11) would not comment, but it is likely that all contracts included such clauses.

Although 68% (34) confirmed they either had or would use auditors and 41% (14) of those expressed a preference for a specialist licensing auditor, the remainder (16) despite having expensive legal contracts, said they would prefer to use informal contact to recover any lost income. Only 26% of organizations questioned had ever invoked audit clauses, and only 4% did so on a regular basis.

Of the companies who exercised audit clauses, 6 confirmed that they had found a significant shortfall, the average under-declaration being 12.5%. Many companies were loathe to put an exact value on recoveries, but some were as high as an additional 20% of declared royalty income. A multinational petroleum company cited an underpayment in excess of $600,000 whilst a computer company reported $240,000 being recovered in a two day audit.

This bizarre situation is as a result of what has been termed a 'trust gap'. Both licensee and licensor have financial control systems, but the licensor has to rely on the control structure in the licensee's company. A staggering 86% (43) relied on the licensee's sales data alone.

This situation is dangerous for both parties. The licensee may have a liability he doesn't know about and the licensor doesn't know whether ROI is accurate.

Methods for Evaluating Intellectual Property Assets

Intellectual property is generated for a whole host of reasons, some of which reflect corporate strategy others a passion for invention. Methods for auditing intellectual property assets include: survey for market pull,

INTELLECTUAL PROPERTY ASSETS	Survey for Market pull	Competitor Analysis	Determine ROI	Audit Agreements	ROI Legal Fees	Survey for Know-how	Analyse Payments
Patent	✔	✔	✔	✔	✔	✔	✔
Copyright	✔	✔	✔	✔	✔	✔	✔
Design Rights	✔	✔	✔	✔	✔	✔	✔
Semiconductor Topography Rights	✔	✔	✔	✔	✔	✔	✔
Trade Secrets	✔	✔	✔	✔	✔	✔	✔
Trade Marks	✔	✔	✔	✔	✔	✔	✔
Service Marks	✔	✔	✔	✔	✔	✔	✔

Figure 8.5 Methods for evaluating intellectual property assets

competitor analysis, ROI, audit of agreements, ROI on legal fees, survey for know-how and analysis of payments, each of which is discussed below.

Survey for Market Pull

This type of activity is typically driven by a company which has decided to license or sell its intellectual property for one reason or another. It reflects methods used by technology brokers whose goal is to locate interested parties to buy or license intellectual property.

A survey for market pull entails developing a number of hypotheses which generate profiles of individuals and companies who would be interested in purchasing a particular item, then mounting a survey to determine if they are interested in buying or not. With careful questioning it's possible to tell the suspect's objection to the purchase. It may be for many reasons which don't disprove the original hypothesis. Of course, this activity needs to be bounded as an exhaustive survey or it will probably have no ultimate point. If no one wants to buy the intellectual property then it has no sale value. At that point other aspects of the asset have to be examined.

Competitor Analysis

From time to time companies file patents, names and so forth, not because they need them but in order to stop a competitor using them. The patent offices are also a source of information on what patents competitors, are filing. Where there is knowledge of a competitor's strategy then patent searching can be informative. Where there is no context in which to view a patent the information is not rich. Ownership of patent gives a state monopoly to the inventor, so it can generate a significant competitive advantage. In filing the patent the invention is disclosed so competitors may know how the invention works, they're just not allowed to use it without the permission of the inventor. To maintain competitive advantage, infringement of intellectual property rights must be vigorously pursued via legal action. Ownership of intellectual property is a right which is only of value when it is exercised.

┌─ IC Concept#21 ───┐

  Protect the Future – Measure Intellectual Property Assets

└──┘

Determine ROI

Determining ROI on intellectual property can be split in many ways. There may be direct benefit such as deploying a patent – in a product the contribution of the intellectual property can be ascribed to the component. There are also intangible benefits derived on the way to discovering a new invention, which will manifest themselves as know-how. Know-how is a human-centred asset which we talk about later in this chapter. IC auditors who begin to travel this path will soon find themselves grappling with the tricky issue of how to determine ROI on research and development. Once again, this can manifest itself in a number of ways dependent upon the goals of the organization.

Not all researchers are sympathetic to the notion of developing an R&D policy in order to satisfy strategic corporate goals. Indeed it is our experience that when R&D managers do try to elicit short, medium and long range goals from senior management they are met with R&D goals that reflect tactical fixes to current market situations. Sometimes the researchers are spot on when developing core technology for the company, as Xerox Parc illustrated with windows, object oriented interfaces, electronic documents and so on which, as it turns out, were not adequately protected as intellectual property of high value.

Audit of Agreements

This topic has been discussed at great length under market assets and it is clear that if the reason for developing and protecting intellectual property is to generate revenue from licensing and other agreements, those agreements must be monitored. The nature of the 'trust gap' has to be identified and managed. In reality, a third party should audit all agreements on the premises of the licensor and check all relevant documents, not just sales data. For example, a software company may have granted a license to a company to sell its software which included five demonstration copies for the showroom. Years later, the licensee changes its policy regarding demonstrations – the two hundred sales staff have laptops and demonstrate the software at the customer's premises. Those copies would not be covered by the original license agreement and a royalty is due and payable. Agreements may not be implemented by those who drew them up, so it's important to check them regularly. Better still, get a third party to do it.

ROI on Legal Fees

Protecting intellectual property can be expensive, especially with worldwide patents to file, maintain and protect. Intellectual property management tends to be undertaken by the department which files and protects patents. It's a specialized type of law. Because the focus of much of this work is protecting it's not proactive from a business perspective. In some cases the revenue generating part of intellectual property and the protecting function are handled by different departments with different goals. It's the role of the IC auditor to bring those two pieces together and examine intellectual property from the aspect of return on investment on legal fees.

Survey for Know-How

If you mounted a survey in your company and asked each employee to list know-how which was valuable to the company, what would the list look like? What percentage of items on the list could be protected as intellectual property and what could not? How would employees in the company know what they are allowed to speak about freely and what should be kept exclusively inside the company? Know-how can be protected as intellectual property under confidentiality or non-disclosure agreements. This type of protection is context dependent. Perhaps a non-disclosure agreement is required when talking to a potential collaborator about a technical joint venture; however, the onus is on the scientist to know in advance that the situation should be treated as confidential and get assistance from legal colleagues to put an agreement in place. Helpful scientists, overjoyed at the opportunity to solve a knotty problem over the phone, are sometimes perplexed at reactions from the intellectual property department who view the situation as giving away a corporate asset, not helping a distressed caller. The extent to which scientists and technical staff are knowledgeable about market and intellectual property is a method of ensuring know-how is protected as intellectual property.

Analysis of Payments

Analysis of payments made from royalty or licensing agreements gives an indication of the value of intellectual property which has been licensed. When auditing licensing and franchise agreements for correct payment, it makes sense to evaluate the payments in the context of the cost of the audit, maintaining the agreement and lost opportunities with alternative licensors and franchisees.

Methods for Evaluating Infrastructure Assets

INFRASTRUCTURE ASSETS	Survey State-of-Art	Determine ROI	Determine fit-for purpose	Determine added value	Interview Customers	Interview Employees	Assess Standards
Management Philosophy	✔		✔	✔	✔	✔	✔
Corporate Culture	✔	✔	✔	✔	✔	✔	
Management Processes	✔	✔	✔	✔	✔	✔	✔
Information Technology Systems	✔	✔	✔	✔	✔	✔	✔
Financial Relations	✔	✔	✔	✔	✔	✔	
Required Standards	✔	✔	✔	✔	✔	✔	✔

Figure 8.6 Methods for evaluating infrastructure assets

Methods for evaluating infrastructure assets are wide ranging, as infrastructure assets include very soft assets like management philosophy and harder ones like computer systems applications.

Survey State-of-the-Art

When looking at infrastructure assets it's important to examine them with respect to what's in place and what's possible. A company which has an old-fashioned management style reflecting power-distance management (telling the troops as little as possible) has to be viewed against alternate management styles and how they would have an impact on the company in question. It's like the hypothesis testing activity which drove the market pull audit for market assets. The IC auditor is asking 'Would this company be more efficient, valuable, whatever if its management style was different?' Understanding the nature of the gap between where the company is and their optimal position means the IC auditor can rank the asset.

It's the same with IT systems. A company may have numerous IT systems in place which are not state-of-the-art. If the systems were improved that might make a difference to services offered, customer satisfaction or lead tracking. Identifying the lost opportunity due to not having state-of-the-art systems gives the IC auditor an indication of relative value.

Determine ROI

Determining ROI on computer systems is fairly straight forward as long as the IC auditor knows the benefits the system was supposed to bring and the benefits can be quantified. Most vendors of IT and networking solutions have ROI as a benefit of the sale. The ROI of the system should be monitored on a regular basis and deployment of new systems may need to be planned years in advance.

Legacy systems, those handed down from one management team to another, can be twenty or thirty years old. Computer code of this age can be very valuable, primarily because the organization may rely on it, its architects have left the company and no one really understands how it works and to throw it away and start over means prohibitive costs.

Changes in management philosophy and processes, such as adoption of Total Quality Management, are reportedly painful and expensive to implement. ROI can eventually be seen in a number of ways, reduction of cost of manufacture, reduction in low quality products and reduction in staff costs. One Black & Decker factory reported a reduction of supervisors from 68 to 20, who were redeployed as business managers.

> IC Concept#22
>
> ## Get the Right Tools – Measure Infrastructure Assets

Determine Fit-for-purpose

'Fit for purpose' determines whether infrastructure assets achieve corporate goals. Working back from goals it's possible to postulate what the organization should look like. This approach is the foundation of re-engineering which seeks to change the organization to focus on delivery of goals. Systems have a persistent quality, especially when their use is reinforced by corporate culture. That's why it's necessary to determine what is fit-for-purpose and discard what isn't.

Determine Added Value

Added value may be derived from infrastructure systems provided the system is appropriately exercised. For example, customer help lines could give valuable feedback to product designers, if the link was put in place. Accounting databases could provide valuable sales tracking mechanisms, if the link was put in place.

Databases

Databases can be very useful and valuable assets provided they are kept up to date. Balancing duplication of data, security and focus always gives infrastructure managers a sore head. For example, accounting databases could provide valuable sales tracking mechanisms, if the appropriate link was put in place. Ways of avoiding the maintenance of databases which are 'nearly perfect' should be put in place. The utilization of databases in the organization has been the subject of thousands of hours of debate and housekeeping effort. The IC auditor will be looking to see if databases are current, fit-for-purpose and used.

Interview Customers

Customers have an unique window on the infrastructure of the organization and their viewpoint should be sought by the IC auditor. Is corporate infrastructure an asset or liability when dealing with the organization in question? Have you ever heard a sales executive who is trying to make a sale look sheepish whilst the potential customer tells them at great length how difficult it is to do business with his company because of all the bureaucracy and procedures? What do they do? Apologize and hope the prospect will take pity on him and give him the sale anyhow – what else?

Interview Employees

Employees have a job to do, not necessarily one which comes with a title, but one which adds value to the organization. Ask them what infrastructure they would feel they require to do a good job, then compare it to the system currently in place. It might be possible to make some simple changes to the infrastructure to add value to the company and make the employee's task easier, more enjoyable and profitable. The IC auditor is looking for the difference between the current and optimal infrastructure systems.

Assess Standards

Assessing standards means both internal and external standards. Having a standard is sadly no guarantee of quality. The job of the IC auditor is not to determine if the standard is adhered to as set out, but whether or not the standard is appropriate for the task in hand. In recent years we have gone standards mad. As you stand in the lobby of an organization it's not unusual to see international standards certificates, quality awards, employee of the month awards and so on, but if the standards don't contribute towards the achievement of corporate goals their value as an asset is low.

Methods for Evaluating Human-centred Assets

As soon as the word assessment or evaluation is used in conjunction with the word staff, adrenaline levels go up. This is a great pity and third millennium companies must seek to redress this negative and pointless situation. The IC auditor will choose a mix of methods which will probably include: interview, test and assess, knowledge elicitation, self-assessment, manager assessment, peer review, and track record assessment.

HUMAN-CENTRED ASSETS	Interview	Test and Assess	Knowledge Elicitation	Self Assessment	Manager Assessment	Peer Review	Assess Record
Education	✔						✔
Vocational Qualifications	✔	✔		✔	✔	✔	
Work Related Knowledge	✔		✔	✔	✔	✔	✔
Occupational Potential	✔	✔					
Personality	✔	✔					
Work Related Competencies	✔		✔	✔	✔	✔	✔

Figure 8.7 Methods for evaluating human-centred assets

Recently, we reviewed a staff appraisal for a part-time bank teller. The employee had been at the same company for more than ten years. Various review criteria were set, accuracy in the till, appearance, whether or not they obeyed a 'greeting' procedure with every customer – smile, look the customer in the eye, refer to them by name. The employee had a perfect track record. She took particular care of her appearance, hair salon once a week, smart clothes and so on. She loved her job and had chosen it because she was a people person, she didn't want to work in the back office. For her the job was about people, they were her customers. In her job appraisal she had a good written review but a less than perfect ranking. When we asked her what she had to do to get a perfect score she didn't know – it had never been discussed. She had no idea how she could improve her performance to get straight As. Neither was she given the opportunity to comment on her manager's performance or that of any of her colleagues. Finally, by way of explanation she announced that her manager had explained that no part-time employees ever got top reviews as it would reflect badly on the full-time employees. She wasn't being reviewed for the right job!

IC Concept#23

Grow People Power – Measure Human-centred Assets

Interview

Interviewing employees is an opportunity to find out exactly what they do, why they do it, their frustrations and so on. The IC auditor will be looking to balance the needs of the organization and the needs of the individual. Some companies choose to have structured interviews, having prepared a discussion paper in advance. The most difficult part of the interview process is getting all parties to believe that the process is supposed to be of mutual benefit and not merely a mechanism to determine if a rise or promotion is due. We promote the viewpoint that an employee is a valuable under-utilized asset and the job of the IC auditor is to identify and help realize the full potential and value of the human asset just as they would an intellectual property or market asset. This means beginning a process of understanding more about what the employee can contribute towards the company even though that might be outside their defined job function.

Test and Assess

Test and assess is a method of finding out more about employees and their potential. There are many companies who offer these services and who will teach others how to manage the testing procedure. Tests have been designed for different attributes, personality, occupational and so forth. Tests must be given by qualified staff and many of the companies also provide training courses for companies wishing to have that expertise in house.

Test results can be shared between employees and in particular we promote an open attitude towards using personality test data as a means of work practices within the organization. A workshop approach works best, as it reinforces the message that there's no right or wrong, good or bad, just the way we are. The IC auditor will be keen to see that employees are given the opportunity to contribute to the organization in as many ways as they wish and are able.

Knowledge Elicitation

Knowledge elicitation is a technique which has evolved over the last twenty years whose aim is to capture the knowledge of an individual so that it can be shared among others and usually finishes up stored in a knowledge base. The idea behind the activity is to provide a capability to replicate human knowledge in areas where it could not previously travel, either because the knowledge was highly specialized, about to be destroyed, or that the environment it needed to be used in was hostile to humans but not to computers, such as in deep space, toxic environments or under the sea. The generic name given to this field, knowledge management, has grown out of Artificial Intelligence research. We talk more about that later. The person performing the knowledge elicitation task is usually working with a particular paradigm which assists in the process of representing the knowledge at a later stage. The IC auditor will be keen to identify knowledge which belongs to key individuals in the company and find ways of capturing and replicating it so that it can be shared throughout the company.

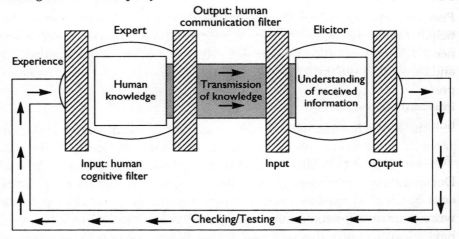

Figure 8.8 Knowledge transmission process (redrawn from Maureen Firlej and Dave Hellens, Knowledge Elicitation, published by Prentice Hall, 1991)

Self-assessment

Assessment processes need to be balanced so we recommend three types self, manager and, where appropriate, peer. Self-assessment gives the employee the chance to review their own success at a particular job function. Assessment can be done to criteria, also chosen with the employee. The whole process should be participative and hopefully that reflects the corporate culture of the organization.

┌─ IC Concept#24 ───

  Management Needs Measurement

Manager Assessment

Self-assessment is followed by manager assessment which forms the basis for discussion with the employee. It's hard to emphasize the importance of getting the tone of these discussions right. Third millennium companies will depend on their ability to position these meetings as mutual discovery, not authoritative assessment. Assessment meetings are also a mechanism to introduce opportunities to use occupational assessment as a way of broadening the scope of the employee's activities in the company and helping them achieve their potential.

Peer Review

Peer assessment is important when individuals work in teams and in participative cultures more of us work in that fashion. Special consideration needs to be given to third millennium work practices such as teleworking and the impact it has on productivity, communication and so forth. Some prefer to undertake peer assessment blind, others sharing not only the information, but also the source. It's very much a cultural issue, but a real hot potato when mismanaged.

Track Record Assessment

Documenting the track record of all employees is a really interesting activity which we have found to be very positive. Just as it's very hard to write your own resumé, it's hard for individuals to recognize what they have learnt and give themselves credit for it. Try this – help an individual that you've known for several years to write their resumé, put in the final finishing touches yourself, then hand it over to them to read. What's the typical reaction? 'I can't do all this' or 'That's not me'. Next, deal with all their objections one by one and by the end of the process the person, says 'Wow, yeah, that really is me!' We're programmed for low self-esteem. The organization needs to market the capabilities of the employee back to the individual by way of keeping a track record of skills, successes and, of course, failures. We have also used 'I can' lists or affirmations to achieve the same goals:

I can develop a marketing strategy.
I can design market research campaigns.
I can manage an international project.
I can develop customer proposals.

I can work well, even under stress
and so on.

What Do You Do When There is No Method?

The first thing to do is look for a similar problem in a different domain
and see how it's solved – then move the method to your domain and see
if it fits. If not invent one. Test it. Fix it. Use it again. The most important
thing to do is document it. Over a period of time a portfolio of methods
evolves which the IC auditor customizes to suit the needs of the situation.
None of the methods we have discussed are new, some are used out of
their usual context. Auditing intellectual capital is a multidisciplinary
task, so developing a number of IC methods for their own sake is silly –
first look around.

5   AUDIT ASPECT

During this step the aspect is audited using one or more methods as
outlined above. We may choose more than one method to audit an aspect
to check our results. For example, if we were interested in value we might
choose both a discounted cash flow method and a market pull method.
After all, in a sales situation assets are not only worth what the company
calculates, but what someone is willing to pay for them.

6   DOCUMENT ASSET VALUE IN IC KNOWLEDGE BASE

Once the aspect has been audited and its status determined and represented as described in the previous chapter, it needs to be kept somewhere. This is called the IC Knowledge Base. The IC Knowledge Base can
be paper based or kept on a computer – we'll talk more about that later.
Because we are always dealing with transitions, the state of the IC
Knowledge Base will be out of date very quickly. Perhaps even before the
audit is complete. It's therefore important to choose a method of keeping
information and knowledge so that it can be regularly updated.

Interpreting the Results of the Audit

Methods of viewing the big picture are essential when looking for trends in intellectual capital. The ultimate goal is to put a financial value on every asset, but there is a useful intermediate step base on indices which helps to see the big picture. This is referred to as indexing.

┌─ IC Concept#25 ──

IC Index = Corporate Health Indicator

Indexing Aspect Values

Every aspect of every asset has an index which can be ranked in a range from 1 to 5, 5 representing its highest value. It doesn't matter that the method of measuring each aspect is different, so long as the relationship between the index and the method of measuring the aspect is defined. In the example shown in Figure 8.9 the asset trade mark is described from the viewpoint of six of its aspects: customer loyalty (to the brand it guards), legal protection, customer recognition, international recognition, international potential, license revenue and stability. Although each aspect has its own method of measurement, its 'state' is always measured as an index between 1 and 5. That mapping will need to be decided by the IC auditor together with company strategists. The index will be unique to the company. So in our example customer loyalty is measured at 40% with an index of 2, because the customer base of that company could reach 90-100%, close to its high values, whereas its International potential may reach 4, as they cover the majority of the European market. This 'gearing' is set, and changes as company strategy and the market also changes.

ASSET: TRADE MARK ASPECT	High Values	Current State	Index (5)
Customer Loyalty	100%	40%	2
Legal Protection	20 year patent	6 years	3
Customer Recognition	100%	60%	4
International Potential	All countries	1	0
License Revenue	$60m	$25m	0
Stability	Competition: none	3	1

Figure 8.9 Indexing aspect values

Coupling

Some aspects have strong relationships with each other, in some cases it may be impossible to have a strong aspect unless another aspect is also strong simultaneously. This bonding of aspects is called coupling. It's important to know which aspects are strongly coupled and which can be independent. Without this knowledge, effort and expense invested in strengthening the index of an aspect can be wasted unless effort is simultaneously spent on another. In the example in Figure 8.10 there are two sets of coupling which have been identified. The first is between customer recognition, international potential and license revenue. The order in which the aspect must be strengthened is indicated by the number in the coupling column. So customer recognition must be strengthened before international potential can be realized and licensing revenue pushed up. This ranks priorities for the IC team who can then work with the marketing department to decide how best to strengthen that particular index.

ASSET: TRADE MARK ASPECT	High Values	Current State	Index (5)	Coupling	
Customer Loyalty	90%	40%	3		
Legal Protection	20 year Patent	6 years	3		↑1
Customer Recognition	90%	60%	4	↑1	
International Potential	Europe	1	0	↓2	
License Revenue	$60m	25	0	↓3	↓2
Stability	No Competition	3	1		

Figure 8.10 Coupling

Monitoring Intellectual Capital via Indices

The performance of indices over time reflects changes in the state of intellectual capital. Figure 8.11 shows how eight aspects of a trade mark asset move. Companies may have a large number of assets which they want to track, so in order to enable us to look at assets at a higher level of abstraction we can generate an average index for an asset by averaging all the aspects which have been graded with an index.

┌─ IC Concept#26 ───
│
│   Constantly Track Intellectual Capital
│
└──

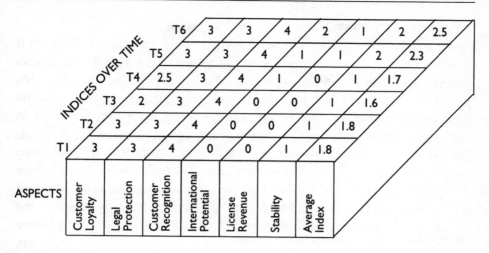

Figure 8.11 Monitoring aspects of an asset via indices

Groups of assets could be ranked in this way and even all market or company assets. The only danger with increasing the granularity of the viewpoint is that aspects with low indices and a coupling of 1 act like the foundation in a house of cards, they can bring the whole house toppling down, so they should not be hidden away and the viewpoint distorted due to lack of detail. An example of this situation would be if the strength of patent protection decreased for some reason, either the patent was challenged, lapsed or expired.

IC Trends and Financial Indicators

Figure 8.12 shows an asset, customer loyalty, which has been tracked over a period of three years. The data for this would have been gathered from customer surveys, designed to indicate the strength of customer loyalty to a particular brand or product. This curve shows that the index began to drop at month eighteen and the event, competitive product, has been identified. The recovery of the index is shown from month 24 onwards. It would be of value to superimpose other curves representing the status of tangible assets such as sales, revenues and so forth to understand the relationship for a particular, brand, company or product. Nasty surprises are in store for companies who fail to understand these relationships which can include the demise of a product, the loss of a work-force and even the failure of the company.

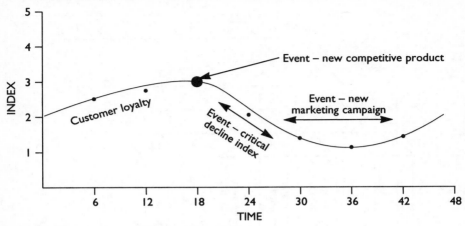

Figure 8.12 Tracking aspects to predict trends

What if the Aspects Rank Really Low?

Having decided on the optimal aspect set, the result of the audit may show huge discrepancies. Instead of repeat business being 100% of customer base it may well be 2%. It's then necessary to look at assets which couple tightly and determine the cause of the problem.

Sadly there are no fixed checklists. The IC auditor has to ask the question 'what other IC assets have an impact on repeat business?'

For example, a proprietary medicine whose aspect state on repeat business was falling should also look at:

Market based assets: brand recognition, customer loyalty
Infrastructure assets: customer satisfaction, networks, distribution
Intellectual property assets: lapsed patents
Human-centred assets: quality of sales force

The IC auditor would look for aspects which couple tightly. This may mean that it's necessary to improve the state of several aspects before a positive impact could be felt on repeat business.

Targeting for Intellectual Capital

Once intellectual capital has been identified that should enable a company to achieve its corporate goals, it's time to look at the target and compare it with the current situation. In order to do this IC assets and their average indices are plotted on a target as shown in Figure 8.13.

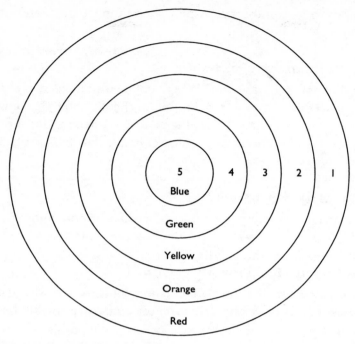

Figure 8.13 Targeting for intellectual capital

The figure is composed of five circles numbered from one to five, five at the centre to reflect the high values associated with the index. Colours are associated with each number:

Red = 1
Orange = 2
Yellow = 3
Green = 4
Blue = 5

A target is constructed for each category of assets and each asset is plotted on the target. Those with an average of 1 a red dot, those with 2 an orange dot and so on. The optimal state is blue so it's easy to get an overall viewpoint of the state of assets.

Big Dots and Little Dots!

Faced with a sea of dots how do you know what's important and what isn't? Answer, have two sizes of dots, large ones for important assets, smaller ones for less important assets, then number them and provide a key.

Finding the Dominant Quadrant

What kind of company are you? When looking at intellectual capital it is possible to determine whether or not particular types of intellectual capital are more important than others. To get a feeling for a dominant quadrant look at the quadrant which contains the greatest number of large dots.

Dominant Market Quadrant

A dominant market company could be a distribution company, or one whose products or services relied on strong branding.

Dominant Intellectual Property Quadrant

A dominant intellectual property company would be one whose products rely on patent and copyright. This type of company probably has a large R&D spend.

Dominant Infrastructure Quadrant

A dominant infrastructure company is one where systems rule, such as a bank or an insurance underwriter.

Dominant Human-centred Quadrant

Here the major asset is the people, so this company is a service company perhaps a consultancy.

Targeting Strengths and Weaknesses

The next step is to look for strengths and weaknesses. Figure 8.14 shows the intellectual capital of a hypothetical company which has plotted the indices of thirty assets on to one target. The target has been split into four quadrants to reflect the four categories of intellectual capital, the dots represent an asset considered by the company to be of value in achieving corporate goals.

There are eight large dots, half are in the intellectual property quadrant. Representing less important assets are 22 smaller dots, eight of which

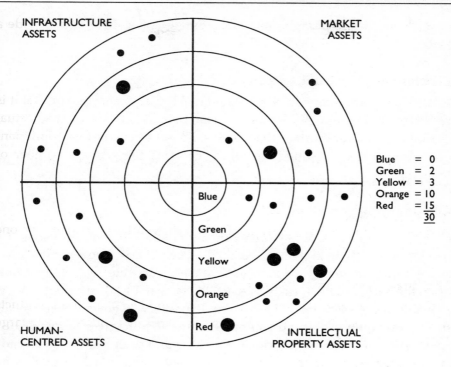

Figure 8.14 Targeting strengths and weaknesses

(36%) are also in the intellectual property quadrant. So this company is an intellectual property dominant company.

The first question is whether or not intellectual property dominance is appropriate. If not then severe changes are required.

Market assets are dispersed with a couple in the green zone but the majority below the average. The infrastructure assets are weak, with 50% ranked in the red zone. 40% of listed assets are intellectual property assets, with 66% below average including all the significant ones. Because of the nature of aspects of intellectual property this does not bode well, as intellectual property tends to weaken over time, not strengthen. So this company, which relies on its intellectual property, is facing the last part of a downward spiral in its intellectual property assets. Human-centred assets are also weak, so we can assume there are no patents or valuable know-how on the horizon. There are no dots in the blue zone. Analysing the spread of the dots:

	Large	Small
Red	3	11
Orange	4	6
Yellow	1	2
Green	0	3
Blue	0	0
Total	**8**	**22**

The intellectual capital of this company looks like it's in pretty bad shape and likely to get worse.

Red Companies

Companies whose assets are predominantly in the red zone are also in the danger zone. Their intellectual capital is very weak and by their own account they are in bad shape to achieve their corporate goals. Depending upon the nature of the weaknesses action needs to be taken straight away, probably short, medium and long-term in parallel. In general there are no short-term solutions for red companies other than to grow inorganically. So acquisition of assets via license, purchase and so on should be considered. Weakness in human-centred assets may reflect a lack of quality or knowledge in the work-force. Time is of the essence here, because red infrastructure, market or human-centred companies probably don't have time to grow to orange or yellow. Red intellectual property dominant companies may decide to buy or license assets.

Orange Companies

Orange companies are too close to the danger zone. Like red companies, orange companies need to mount actions which are short medium and long-term to push them towards blue. Ranking of activities should be made by considering coupling of aspects and determining the critical path for intellectual capital growth. Orange infrastructure and market dominated companies have probably run out of time to grow organically. Orange human-centred and intellectual property dominated companies may have time to either hire new staff and buy or license assets.

Yellow Companies

Yellow can be good or bad depending on which way the trend is going. Yellow companies need to focus on measurement to make sure the company is really on the edge of safety zones and must know what short-term trends will ensure they either remain orange or become green.

Green Companies

Green companies are in pretty good shape, yet they have not achieved their goals. If they have been blue before, their ability to sustain that position has been eroded by some factor. Are measures in place to fix that situation? If not, they can expect to be yellow pretty soon, then there might not be time to fix the situation before it becomes unrecoverable. Green companies should already have an intellectual capital policy in place and have regular audits and reviews.

Blue Companies

Blue is best. Blue companies have set targets and achieved them. Now it's time to reset targets and grow. Bobbing about from blue to green as a result of re-targeting is healthy as long as it's controlled. Blue companies should be planning long and medium term to expand their intellectual capital.

Determine Improvement Strategy

How the state of an asset can be improved is dependent upon the nature of the asset and the aspect. For example, improving brand awareness in China of a soft drink could employ a number of promotion mechanisms:

1 Give a can of soft drink to every person in China
2 Launch a radio campaign
3 Launch a TV campaign
4 Identify a hero in China to endorse the product
5 Run extensive advertising in the press
6 Make it cheaper than all alternative soft drinks
7 Make it more expensive than all alternative soft drinks
8 Give it away free with a product all Chinese people may buy

and so on, it depends on the market strategy for the soft drink.

Organic Versus Inorganic Growth

If an aspect has a poor state which means that it can't contribute to the status of transition desired, then the next decision is how to acquire the asset, develop it, that is organically, or acquire it – inorganically. Again, this depends on how tightly coupled the asset is with other assets. If acquisition is the answer, then ideally the asset should be loosely coupled with other assets. For example, patents sometimes don't travel well from one company to another if there is complex know-how associated with its implementation or manufacture into a product. That means the person who invented the patent may have to travel with the patent as well. Sadly, this is often the reason intellectual property is not exploited more extensively in the market, as the employer would rather drop a patent and not license it to another company, than lose either the employee or his time. The company may decide it's better for inventors to spend their time generating new inventions which would benefit the company, rather than have to sell their time or lose them as an employee.

Organic growth means the company will develop or fix the state of the asset themselves. This can be a very time consuming business, as it may mean expensive investment in marketing programmes, infrastructure building and design or financing R&D programmes to generate new intellectual property. The route to acquisition will always be determined by time and available financial resources.

Should Assets Determine Strategy?

Consider the predicament of a new editor taking over a magazine. He has aspirations to expand the business and take a prominent place in the market. After a couple of months he discovers that he doesn't have a stable of writers who could achieve corporate goals. He has decided to examine his assets to determine where the magazine's strengths are, then build the business based on those strengths. Is that a good idea? This is a question we are often asked, do you build on your strengths or acquire new ones. The answer depends on the required transition. If the goal is to keep a group of journalists in employment, then it doesn't really matter what they write on, management, baby care, food, provided there is a market for the product. If the goal of the publisher is to have a top ranking management magazine and he has a stable of mediocre journalists, then the goal is not achievable with those assets. Maybe he moves the mediocre journalists to a mediocre magazine, freeing up capital for investing in a new stable of journalists. It's a matter of ranking goals and choosing transitions.

Asset Checklist

Market Assets
Service Brands
Product Brands
Corporate Brands
Champions
Customers
Evangelists
Customer Loyalty
Repeat Business
Company Name
Backlog
Distribution Channels
Business Collaborations
Franchise Agreements
Licensing Agreements
Favourable Contracts

Intellectual Property Assets
Patent
Copyright
Computer Software

Design Rights
Trade Secrets
Know-how
Trade marks
Service marks

Human-centred Assets
Education
Vocational Qualifications
Work Related Knowledge
Work Related Competencies

Infrastructure Assets
Management Philosophy
Corporate Culture
Management Processes
Impact of Information
Technology Systems
Networking Systems
Financial Relations
Required Standards

IC Audit Questions

- Have we agreed the transition required for the company to meet its objectives?
- Have we specified the domains to be addressed and documented any relevant constraints?
- Is there a defined optimal aspect set?
- What is the coupling between these aspects?
- What methods will be used?
- Which measures will be applied to the results?

9

Intellectual Capital Management

When intellectual capital has initially been identified, indexed and activities for the development, management and acquisition of new intellectual capital identified, the process of intellectual capital management takes over. The process, as illustrated in Figure 9.1, is broken down in to seven activities, each of which is described below. The intellectual capital audit and the development of policy are really iterative tasks because it's difficult to develop a policy in a vacuum, but for the purposes of clarity they are treated as if they are serial tasks.

- Identify intellectual capital
- Develop an intellectual capital policy
- Audit intellectual capital
- Document and store in the intellectual capital knowledge base
- Guarding of intellectual capital
- Growth and renewal of intellectual capital
- Disseminate

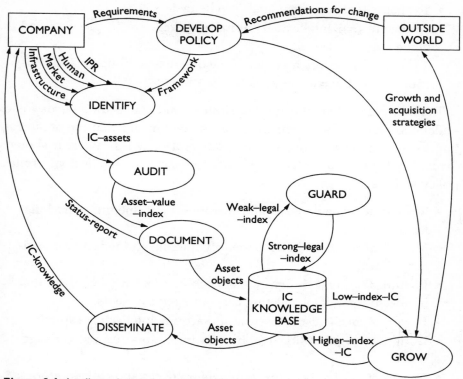

Figure 9.1 Intellectual capital management process

Identify Intellectual Capital

Is the first step in understanding the nature and content of the intellectual capital of the organization. Organizations may have a lot of intangible assets but still be poor in intellectual capital.

┌─ IC Concept#27 ──────────────────────────────────
│
│   Intellectual Capital = Corporate Sustainability
│
└──

Develop an Intellectual Capital Policy

Once the organization understands the nature of its intellectual capital, a policy is required for growing and maintaining it. The objectives of the intellectual capital policy are:

- To ensure that corporate goals can be met.
- To ensure that intellectual capital resources are in place as and when they are needed.
- To ensure that every member of the organization understands this process and the part they play in its success.

The interplay between corporate strategy and goal setting needs to be understood and defined. Separation of the two means that the organization loses track of which assets it needs and of which assets it should divest itself. Tasks undertaken in order to design the intellectual capital policy include:

- Review of strategic goals and threats – short, medium and long-term.
- Identification of methods to identify missing and redundant intellectual capital.
- Identification and design of feedback mechanisms to ensure that intellectual capital is meeting corporate requirements.
- Design of mechanisms to grow and acquire intellectual capital.
- Design of organizational policy on intellectual capital management.
- Design of mechanisms for training employees and collaborators.

Mechanisms to Review Strategic Goals and Threats

Policy recommendations here could include the establishment of a group of individuals whose P&L responsibility depended upon intellectual capital being in place when the company needed it. Their function might be to regularly review a prepared intellectual capital report showing trends and compare the evolving situation to the needs of the company.

Methods to Identify Missing and Redundant Intellectual Capital.

Methods to identify missing intellectual capital could also include a status report on intellectual capital not yet mature. An intellectual capital road map could be drawn up and used to evaluate the status of intellectual capital in the organization.

There may be intellectual capital in the company which the company does not use, or could generate incremental income from via new commercial arrangements. Policy could recommend the use of an external organization to generate such revenue or appoint an individual in the company to perform that function.

Design of Feedback Mechanisms

Feedback mechanisms are required in order to ascertain if the policies put in place are having the desired effect on the state of intellectual capital in the organization. An example of feedback mechanisms could be review meetings to assess the progress of the IC policy.

Mechanisms to Develop and Acquire Intellectual Capital

Guidelines need to be put in place to determine how the decision to develop and acquire new intellectual capital will be made. Great care needs to be taken to avoid the NIH (not invented here) trap. A general reticence to license intellectual property, products and services is a huge waste of money and opportunity for all concerned. Policies which recommend the evaluation of organic versus inorganic acquisition methods should be discussed.

Organizational Policy on Intellectual Capital Management

An organizational policy on intellectual capital should be put in place to ensure that those charged with intellectual capital management have both the responsibility and authority to perform their designated functions.

Training Employees and Collaborators

Once the organizational policy has been designed it should be merchandised to both employees and collaborators. An education programme would help both merchandise the policy and help all concerned understand their role and added value in the programme.

Audit Intellectual Capital

The mechanics of the intellectual capital audit have already been explained in great detail but from a management perspective mechanisms need to be put in place to ensure that the audit is not just an exercise. The management process should include a status report on intellectual capital and recommendations for intellectual capital restructuring.

Document and Store in the Intellectual Capital Knowledge Base

Companies who are serious about deriving maximum benefit from their intellectual capital need to plan to store information and knowledge about their intellectual capital on a computer system where those who require access can have their own interface customized. The use of a computer system to store complex know-how is a particularly good idea. However, its design will need to respond to user requirements and those can only be defined once the application is fully understood by the user. So before investing in computerization a paper system is the best idea.

Starting with Paper

Using the diagrammatic approach outlined throughout this book a start can be made on documenting intellectual capital. The documentation process will eventually get out of hand as the scope of the exercise gets under way, but the intellectual capital management team should try to document as wide a spectrum of intellectual capital as possible in order to fully understand what they will want from their eventual system.

Building the Intellectual Capital Knowledge Base

Once the intellectual capital of the organization has been identified and a paper system has been under trial for a while, the management team may consider it appropriate to manage it via computer. In order to keep track of IC, the organization will need to maintain an intellectual capital knowledge base. Tasks in building the IC knowledge base include:

- Design of the intellectual capital knowledge base
- Design of the user interfaces
- Population of the intellectual capital knowledge base
- Training of intellectual capital knowledge base administration staff
- In-house training programme on the use of intellectual capital within the organization

Design of the Intellectual Capital Knowledge Base

The design of the intellectual capital knowledge base, like all other computer systems, needs to be characterized by the eventual user. If the management of intellectual capital is new to the organization and it will be for most, then the successful use of a paper system is an essential pre-requisite. The diagrammatic method as outlined in this book is a good basis for the design of the system, but much will depend on how the system is to be used in the organization. The richest use of intellectual capital is to provide knowledge by those who already possess it to those who need it but don't have it. This situation has been characterized by those building expert systems over the last twenty years. The way the knowledge base is designed will depend upon the organizations plans for its eventual use. There are many knowledge-based shells which may be purchased 'off the shelf' should their structure be suitable. Knowledge auditors will not concern themselves with the inner workings of the knowledge base, as that issue falls in to the domain of corporate infra-structure, so the individual who would normally be responsible for the acquisition of all IT infrastructure software would be the person to make the eventual choice of knowledge-based system design.

Design of the User Interfaces

Several individuals will want to examine the intellectual capital knowl-edge base for various reasons. Each type of user will require their own user interface which provides a helpful window on the information for the individual. Executives will require summary information, knowledge management professionals will require interfaces which permit them to modify and change the knowledge base with ease. The design of the user interface and the knowledge base is an expert task which will mean that outside help will probably be required by most companies.

Population of the Intellectual Capital Knowledge Base

This task concerns typing knowledge and information which has been discovered in the organization into the knowledge base. It is likely that an interface will be built which asks questions of the person whose job is to populate the knowledge base so the task does not have to be a straight typing task.

Training of Intellectual Capital Knowledge Base Administration Staff

Like all other systems, the intellectual capital knowledge base will require support and maintenance. An important infrastructure asset in its own right the intellectual capital knowledge base will need to have tight security and access control. Organizations will find it convenient to add the function of intellectual capital knowledge base administrator to the intellectual capital management team.

In-house Training Programme on the Use of Intellectual Capital Within the Organization.

Like all computer systems, they will fail without proper introduction to the people who will ultimately use them. This activity should concern itself with how best to introduce the new system and the education programme for its users.

Guarding of Intellectual Capital

Guarding of intellectual capital is concerned with the protection of intellectual, market, human and infrastructure assets. Each type of intellectual capital requires different types of protection and has associated professionals who are the best individuals to undertake the task. We discuss each category briefly below.

┌─ IC Concept#28 ──────────────────────────────────────┐

Differentiate Through Intangibles

└──┘

Guarding Market Assets

Market assets are guarded by intellectual property rights and by mechanisms for 'feeding' them, such as advertising for trade marks, and promotions for company name.

Guarding Intellectual Property Assets

Intellectual property assets are guarded by registration of patent, trade marks, design rights and, in some countries, copyright. Trade secrets are guarded by confidentiality agreements.

Guarding Human-centred Assets

Human-centred assets are guarded by growth opportunities in well-rewarded and interesting work which provides the employee with job satisfaction and the knowledge that their position represents a worthy contribution to the enterprise. This is a much more difficult task than guarding any other type of asset, but worth the extra effort as they provide the greatest value.

Guarding Infrastructure Assets

Infrastructure assets are guarded in part by management who dictate philosophy and design management processes, which in turn dictate corporate culture. Other assets are guarded by measures which ensure security of IT systems

Growth and Renewal of Intellectual Capital

Growth and renewal of intellectual capital is a large topic and is the focus of the next chapter. The intellectual capital management team is not responsible for the growth itself, but for its management to ensure it complies with organizational policy.

Dissemination

The responsibility for dissemination of information about intellectual capital by way of know-how is the responsibility of the IC management team. Feedback mechanisms should indicate how successful their role is. The major methods of dissemination will be via use of the knowledge base or via the intellectual capital report.

The Intellectual Capital Management Team

In order to perform the above mentioned tasks, expertise from several disciplines is required, including:

Strategic Management Expertise

Strategic management expertise is required to identify and develop hierarchies of goals and understand how the management philosophy, processes and corporate culture can best be used as intellectual capital. They are also required to make recommendations for the restructuring of intellectual capital.

Intellectual Property Management Expertise

Intellectual property management expertise is required to determine how best to protect and manage intellectual property using patent law and provide expertise to evaluate patents and so on.

Marketing Expertise

Marketing expertise is required to identify business opportunities originating from all forms of intellectual capital assets, devise strategies and to grow, acquire and add value to various market assets.

Information Technology Management Expertise

Information technology expertise is required to identify how best to provide IT systems which mirror infrastructure requirements of the organization. In addition, expertise is required to evaluate the impact infrastructure assets such as groupware, use of Internet and so forth has on the organization.

Human Resource Expertise

Human resource expertise is required to ensure that the organization hires, manages and grows valuable assets which are optimally used within the company. In addition, there is a requirement to identify expertise outside the company when there is a need, either by way of subcontractors or part-time employees.

Recruiting the Intellectual Capital Management Team

Most of the expertise required already exists within the company, but to put the intellectual capital management team together some changes may be required. These staff functions have probably not worked together to manage intangible assets in this new context. There may also be some changes in the way management of resources occurs, most notably trading reactive practices for proactive ones.

IC Concept#29

IC Management is a Continual Process

IC Management Team Audit Questions

- What are the important elements of IC for our company?
- Do we have an explicit policy to manage and improve the IC knowledge base?
- Are there mechanisms to identify missing and redundant IC, with respect to our corporate goals?
- Who will use the IC knowledge base, and how will they be trained?
- How will we report the state of our IC knowledge base to shareholders and other stakeholders?

10

Knowledge Management and Corporate Memory

The UK Patent Office tells this story on their promotional road shows: A British chemical company was developing a process which they had perfected at the pilot plant level. When the process was scaled up to full production an unwanted sludge was produced in the bottom of the reaction vessel. As a result of this residue the company was contemplating a programme of research to try and eliminate the problem. A researcher had noticed an advertisement for the Patent Office's Search and Advisory Service. So before embarking on a costly programme they made an enquiry via the service, to see if a UK company had experienced a similar problem and had developed a solution from which they might learn or alternatively license it. The Patent Office mounted a search and located a patent which proved to be the perfect solution.

The patented process had been developed some years earlier and patented by guess who – themselves!

This story is not the only one, indeed in the *Financial Times* on February 21st 1996, an article written by Tom Lester begins with a story about an oil company which was about to mount a seismic survey in the Gulf of Mexico when an executive remembered 'in the nick of time' that they had not only surveyed the area before but had also drilled some inconclusive wells. His memory had saved the company quite a lot of money. How often does this happen and why?

Of all the types of intellectual capital to manage, knowledge management is the most complex and therefore deserves a chapter to discuss its peculiarities.

The subject of knowledge management has been around for a very long time. Its roots lie in artificial intelligence (AI), whose goals have been to synthesize human behaviour with computers. Pamela McCorduck's book *Machines who Think* gives a very readable overview of the growth of research in this area spanning the last fifty years.

Human problem-solving has always been a seductive area for AI researchers as it forms the basis for the majority of systems. Even tasks as outwardly trivial as vacuuming a room require an understanding of what is garbage, what is furniture, what can be moved, what can't, the best route around the room and so on. That's why in this age of microelectronics we don't have robots to assist in the house yet. In order to build a machine which could even emulate, let alone synthesize, the behaviour of humans considerable effort is needed to understand how we acquire, manipulate and store knowledge. Systems which do this are called knowledge based, not just because they keep knowledge, but because the way in which they manipulate knowledge inside the machine is different to the way a conventional system, such as stock control or payroll, works. Incidentally that's also why the repository we have chosen to store knowledge about intellectual capital is a knowledge base not a database.

There are two groups of researchers who are interested in knowledge management, one representing pull, the other push – so that's quite healthy. We have already mentioned the push faction – the artificial intelligence group – who are seeking to provide answers to the problem of managing knowledge. They typically use computers as a tool – some because knowledge is complex and huge and computers are a useful tool to manage it, others because their interest is in making computers think like humans. Their goals are different, but the research both undertake contributes towards the solution of the harder problem – how to understand and manage knowledge.

The pull group are those from the classical management domain, who are interested in knowledge management because they perceive it to be such a huge corporate asset. Skimming the contents page of a book entitled 'Knowledge Management' will give an indication of which group the writer belongs to – describing the problem or trying to answer it. Collaboration between these two communities has already begun. Examples include Karl Wiig who runs his Knowledge Management consulting business from Arlington, Texas, and The Technology Broker in Cambridge UK.

The Dutch Management Network

In 1994 the Dutch Management Network, in which several companies and professionals exchange experiences in the field of knowledge management, held a survey covering 80 organizations. Its main goal was to investigate the following questions:

- What are the opinions of managers about the relationship between performance of business processes and knowledge?
- How effective are current policies in the area of knowledge management?
- What are the main bottlenecks with regard to the use and development of knowledge within organizations?

Some of the remarkable results of this survey were:

- 52% of the respondents reported difficulties in securing knowledge when persons were transferred or when business processes were restructured
- 57% of the respondents reported costly mistakes because of the fact that knowledge was not available at the place and/or point in time when it was needed
- 80% of the respondents reported critical business processes in which knowledge was only available to one or two persons.

Source: Rob van der Spek

┌─ IC Concept#30 ───┐
│   │
│   Put Knowledge Into Every Process   │
│   │
└──┘

KNOWLEDGE AND INFORMATION

Before we move on to a more detailed discussion of knowledge management, the distinction between knowledge and information needs to be made explicit. In his trilogy on knowledge management, Karl Wiig lays the foundation for thinking about corporate knowledge. His definitions clearly illustrate the difference between knowledge and information…

> Knowledge consists of truths and beliefs, perspectives and concepts, judgments and expectations, methodologies and know-how. Knowledge is accumulated, organized and integrated and held over longer periods to be available to be applied to handle specific situations and problems. Information consists of facts and data that are organized to describe a particular situation or problem.
> Knowledge is subsequently applied to interpret the available information about a particular situation and to decide how to handle it.
>
> *Karl Wiig*

When considering mounting a knowledge management strategy it is important to focus on why the programme is put in place as managing all types of knowledge may not be either practical or required, so understanding the types of knowledge used in the company and their relative importance is recommended.

What is Knowledge Management?

Knowledge management comprises all the activities as outlined in the intellectual capital management process, but the process as applied to knowledge management is more complex than when it's applied to intellectual property or market assets. To illustrate the difference we shall look inside each process of the intellectual capital process as illustrated again below.

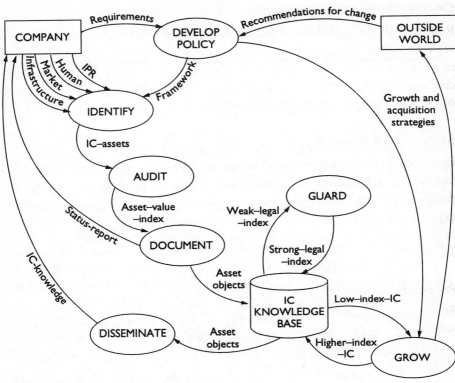

Figure 10.1 The knowledge management process

Identification of Knowledge

The first step is to identify knowledge which can be considered as an asset. At some level all knowledge is an asset, even knowing how to send a fax, so to avoid looking at every piece of knowledge in the company we shall start by looking at Wiig's levels of knowledge.

Levels of Knowledge

Knowledge can be split in to four conceptual levels:

- Goal-setting or idealistic knowledge
- Systematic knowledge
- Pragmatic knowledge
- Automatic knowledge

Goal-Setting or Idealistic Knowledge

Refers to vision, goal and paradigm knowledge. Part of this knowledge is well known to us and explicit – we work consciously with it. However, most of it is not well known, it is tacit – and only accessible non-consciously. We use this knowledge to identify what is possible to create our goals and values, (knowledge WHY).

Systematic Knowledge

Refers to system, schema and reference methodology knowledge. Our theoretical knowledge of underlying systems, general principles and problem-solving strategies to approach situations is to a large extent explicit and well known to us. We use this knowledge to analyse a reason in depth and to synthesize new approaches and alternatives, (knowledge THAT).

Pragmatic Knowledge

Refers to decision making and factual knowledge. Decision making knowledge is practical and mostly explicit. We use this knowledge to perform our daily work and to make explicit decisions, (knowledge HOW).

Automatic Knowledge

Refers to automated working knowledge. We are so familiar with this knowledge that we have automated it – most has become tacit. We use it to perform tasks automatically – without conscious reasoning.

Using the four categories of knowledge listed above it is possible to categorize knowledge which is of interest to us. The process of knowledge identification is only interesting when the type of knowledge we consider is identified and categorized. It may be that over a period knowledge which used to be well documented and shared has become tacit, moving from the few to the many, enriching the organization and enabling them to perform their jobs in a more knowledgeable way. Or it could be the opposite, once widely shared knowledge has ceased to be recreated and is now only known by a few. It's important to understand the status and the trend in order to formulate an appropriate plan. Organizations who realize they rely on a large amount of pragmatic knowledge may find that methods of sharing factual information increases the quality of employee performance in the work environment. The type of knowledge which is of value will determine the techniques which are used in order to capture and document it.

Granularity and Proficiency

Granularity, proficiency and criticality are other aspects of knowledge to consider. Granularity of knowledge refers to the size of the knowledge chunk which is required to undertake a particular job. If a company is a management consultancy then different members of staff would be proficient in manipulating knowledge chunks at different levels of granularity and proficiency. Consider the domain of conducting a market survey. A senior member of staff may understand how to plan and undertake all aspects of the survey, from planning to performing it, whereas a junior member of staff may only know how to perform a small piece of the operation, such as conducting a telephone interview. The intellectual capital auditor needs to understand where everybody fits on a scale which is meaningful to the requirements of the company. This type of scale would be similar in function to the NVQ scale, showing a hierarchy of domain knowledge and proficiency in applying it.

Figure 10.2 shows a span of knowledge for three domains and provides a terminology for knowledge span.

IC Concept#31

Know About Your Corporate Knowledge

Once we have some idea of the types of knowledge and the granularity in which it manifests itself with job functions, it is necessary to examine proficiency. Figure 10.3 shows how individuals could be ranked according to their competence and performance based on the percent of domain knowledge they have and use. Competence refers to the degree of understanding based on available knowledge. It's knowledge of knowledge, they understand what's needed to perform the job. Those who just perform the job may not understand theoretical aspects of the job but are proficient and may perform the job day in day out. Performance knowledge means that they use their knowledge to actually do the job, not necessarily reasoning about why or how they are performing it.

Knowledge Span	Examples
Knowledge Domain	Domains of: • Internal Medicine • Mechanical Engineering • Business Management; etc.
Knowledge Region	Regions of: • Urology • Automotive Mechanical Design and Engineering • Product Marketing; etc.
Knowledge Section	Sections of: • Kidney Diseases • Transmission Design • New Product Planning; etc.
Knowledge Segment or Reference Case	Segments or 'Cases' of: • Diagnosis of Kidney Diseases • Gear Train Specification and Design • Product Marketability Evaluations; etc. Specific Reference Case of: • Diagnosing Mrs. Smith's kidney stone with its complications; etc.
Knowledge Element	Elements of: • Diagnostic strategies. such as 'When considering which disease is present, first collect all symptoms, then try to explain as many of them as possible with one disease candidate' • Gear Train Contact Force and Energy Loss Calculations • Customer Acceptance Estimations; etc.
Knowledge Fragment	Fragments of: 'If the symptom is excruciating pain, then consider kidney stone' 'When there are too many gears in the transmission, the energy loss will be excessive' 'When there are many comparable and competitive products already in the marketplace, a new product must offer very special and attractive features to be highly competitive'; etc.
Knowledge Atom	Atoms of: 'One symptom is excruciating pain'; 'Use case hardening of gear surfaces in pressure range 4'; 'Price is a negative competitive factor in most cases'; etc.

Figure 10.2 Span of knowledge (redrawn from Karl M. Wiig, Knowledge Management Foundation, published by Schema Press, 1993)

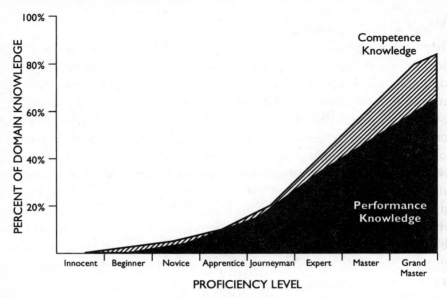

Figure 10.3 A hypothetical model for how competence and performance knowledge may grow with increasing proficiency (redrawn from Karl M Wiig, Knowledge Management Foundation, published by Schema Press, 1993)

Identify Critical Knowledge Functions

Critical knowledge functions are business functions that typically involve knowledge intensive work that cannot easily be performed by available suitable personnel or be readily automated. This may be because:

- The required knowledge is rare, few people possess it
- It's largely tacit and therefore difficult to document
- It hasn't been identified as critical

The reader is probably beginning to realize that the subject of knowledge management is huge, which indeed it is. Deciding to mount a knowledge management programme for an entire company is not a starting point we would recommend. A wiser approach is to try to determine where the critical knowledge functions within a company are, then focus on enriching them or expanding the number of people in the company who can perform them. At a minimum, it is necessary to be able to identify and prioritize critical knowledge functions to ensure the organization's ability to perform them is not reduced or destroyed by badly planned re-engineering programmes.

Audit Knowledge

There are numerous types and levels of knowledge, far too many to include in an overview book of this nature. So when examining knowledge and its management in the company from an audit perspective, we are looking at the nature and type of knowledge and where it is used, not used, or missing within the company. The management philosophy and corporate culture of the organization in question will have an impact on how much knowledge should filter through the company. Companies with a power-distance culture will promote dissemination on a need to know basis, while participative cultures are more willing to share knowledge throughout the company. This is a question every CEO must address when steering the company. Knowledgeable workers are more likely to be able to act intelligently than those kept in the dark. The management challenge is in identifying the optimal knowledge required for any employee to perform the optimal job.

Document the Knowledge

It is our goal to document knowledge about intellectual capital, for which we recommend the use of knowledge based systems. However, it is not our goal to document the knowledge which comprises part of human-centred assets. For example, if the knowledge a company needs in order to function is how to design aeroplanes, we will document knowledge about the design of aeroplanes as it pertains to that company – who possesses it, their level of competence and performance, whether it is tacit, and so on. We will not document or model the knowledge on designing aeroplanes itself using a computer. Yet.

What's in Your Corporate Memory?

Corporate memory is an organic entity. It's a decentralized unpredictable life form comprising multiple independent memories that can die, desert the critical mass at any time to join a competitor or just leave because it felt like it. We believe that knowledge is too valuable to third millennium enterprises to treat in this way. Corporate memory is a concept yet to be realized, as currently memory does not belong to the corporation but to the body of individuals who work there. As the requirements of industry are increasingly knowledge based it is to their advantage to try to take ownership of the knowledge of the work-force. That could be done by generating a memory which was persistent, that is, it existed independently of the work-force. Corporate memory is the ultimate goal of the documentation of intellectual capital, as then the asset has moved from the domain of the human to the machine. That's not to say that documenting knowledge is an all or nothing task and the IC auditor should initially be concerned with documenting meta-knowledge, that is, knowledge about knowledge until we are able to efficiently document knowledge itself.

┌─ IC Concept#32 ─────────────────────────────────────

Build a Corporate Memory

└──

Disseminate the Knowledge

Knowledge can be explicit, tacit or implicit. Tacit knowledge is internalized and therefore not readily available for transfer to another. Tacit knowledge is frequently of huge value within the organization so the fact that it is not readily transferable is inconvenient from the perspective of the organization. Explicit knowledge is available as it has been formalized in our heads, or documented in books and papers. Therefore it can be disseminated via discussion, being taught, being read and so on. Knowledge may also be implicit, which means it is hidden inside procedures, management practices or even in the corporate culture.

In order to ease the dissemination, the organization should seek to increase the amount of explicit knowledge they have available. This also means that steps have to be taken to make implicit and tacit knowledge explicit. This can be achieved by working with owners of tacit knowledge to help them make their knowledge explicit thus enabling its dissemination more easily.

Developing a Policy for Knowledge Management

A policy for knowledge management must fit in with the corporate culture and management philosophy of the company. Shared knowledge is an aspect of a participative management philosophy. Individuals may

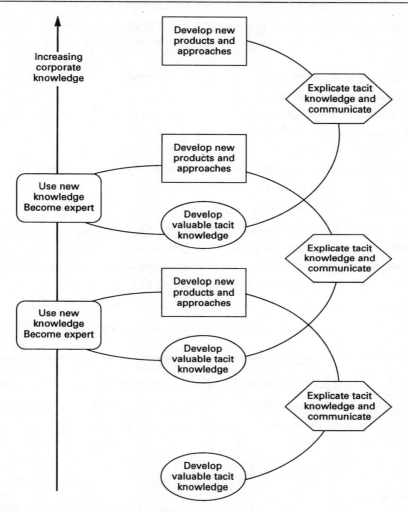

Figure 10.4 Conceptual illustration of the knowledge spiral

be less than co-operative in sharing knowledge if they perceive loss of personal knowledge to be a precursor for loss of their job. We anticipate that in the third millennium a new framework describing the employment of the individual will be called for by knowledge based workers. A policy for knowledge management would need to include prioritization of knowledge for identification and a statement on the ethical basis upon which knowledge elicited from the individual can be used, disseminated and exploited. The future of knowledge management brings a new dimension to 'intellectual property management'.

Developing the Corporate Knowledge Base

Knowledge can be developed in a number of ways:

- Additional education
- Additional training
- Reading books and papers
- Learning from the media and electronic networks
- On the job learning
- Learning through experiences
- Research and development
- Personnel innovation

In order to play a meaningful role in the knowledge management process, knowledge growth should be encouraged which can add value to the assets of the organization and enhance the organization's ability to achieve its corporate goals, but more about that in the next chapter.

```
┌─ IC Concept#33 ─────────────────────────────────────┐
│          Knowledge Means Power and Profits           │
└──────────────────────────────────────────────────────┘
```

A Last Word on Knowledge Management

Knowledge management, like other parts of intellectual capital management, is a topic in its own right. However, it is emerging as an area of interest to corporate strategists who are turning to the research community for answers to some complex questions. Our discussion here has been cursory and is intended as a catalyst to begin the process of thinking about the role and value of knowledge in the corporation and the way it is used.

Knowledge Management Audit Questions

- What are the critical knowledge functions in our company?
- Who possesses this knowledge?
- What is our policy for managing and disseminating knowledge?
- How could we promote knowledge sharing within the company?
- To what extent does the operation of the company rely on tacit knowledge?
- What measures can we take to turn tacit knowledge into explicit knowledge?
- What steps can we take to protect our corporate knowledge?

‖
Extending the Intellectual Capital Asset Base

Extending the intellectual capital asset base can be achieved in several ways, but the optimal situation is to have a company which is so rich in ideas that the intellectual capital management process has a hard time keeping up with the company. Those who have ever worked in a really exciting company know what that feels like. Creativity and innovation abound everywhere in the company. In marketing, manufacturing or the R&D labs, wondrous things always seem to be happening. There is a feeling of success and of constant movement and change. Such are the experiences of those who have worked for some Silicon Valley startups. Why aren't all companies like that? What is it about these companies which enables them to grow, become successful and also become very valuable?

One obvious factor is the youth and energy of the employees, in terms of age. Information technology is an industry which employs a lot of young people. But these young people are running the show, they are not the support staff and they are there 7am until late at night, every day – why?

CREATING A CULTURE FOR CHANGE

If the management philosophy and management processes are designed to encourage employees to confront problems head on and tackle change as part of the daily challenge, a corporate culture evolves to help employees do that. The company heroes are those who excel in the process and help the company to win and grow. What we are talking about is creating a corporate culture which promotes and supports the process of innovation.

Poor on Innovation – Poorer in Intellectual Capital

There is a direct relationship between how innovative a company is and its ability to expand intellectual capital. Innovation in marketing strategies, branding, thinking of things to license, in R&D, in the use and design of infrastructure and in the ways we challenge and grow employees to mutual advantage. Innovative companies are rich in intellectual capital, and their culture and philosophy is a rich environment for the continual enrichment of the intangible assets of a company. Before we talk about specific methods for expanding intellectual capital it's appropriate to talk about innovation and creativity within the organization.

Innovation is about ideas, and the process of turning them in to reality. If employees constantly look to their leaders for new ideas and ways to bale them out of situations, they are not contributing to the growth and life of a company. The degree to which a company is innovative is a measure of its life force. Companies lacking in innovation are experiencing their final death throws before they are buried by the competition. If there is a general reticence for all employees to be innovative and contribute towards growth, change and success in the organization then the management philosophy and the processes should be examined to see how they can be changed to embrace the concept of innovation as a way of life. There are several methods which have been written about in recent years which are of use when it's time to break old habits and come up with something new.

Six Thinking Hats

Edward De Bono's 'Six Thinking Hats' is a great method to use in a brainstorming session and one which we have used on many occasions successfully. The basic idea is to 'unscramble thinking so that a thinker is able to use one thinking mode at a time – instead of trying to do everything at once' The six thinking hats are each represented by a colour:

- White Hat: virgin white, pure facts, figures and information.
- Red Hat: seeing red, emotions and feelings, also hunch and intuition.
- Black Hat: devil's advocate, negative judgement, why it will not work.
- Yellow Hat: sunshine, brightness and optimism, positive, constructive, opportunity.
- Green Hat: fertile, creative, plants sprinkling from seeds, movement, provocation.
- Blue Hat: cool and control, orchestra conductor, think abut thinking.

During a brainstorming session participants must all wear the same 'colour hat' until ideas run dry, then you move on to the next colour, depending upon what type of thinking is required next. De Bono explains the Six Thinking Hats method in detail in his book of the same name which we recommend readers evaluate to see if it could play a role in helping to develop new intellectual capital in the company.

A Kick in the Seat of the Pants

And a Whack on the Side of the Head are both book titles by Roger von Oech whose purpose is also to help us break out of old thinking patterns and use roles to help identify new thinking behaviour which is required to solve particular problems. His roles include:

- The Explorer: when it's time to seek out new information, get off the beaten path, poke around in outside areas and pay attention to unusual patterns.
- The Artist: when you need to create a new idea, ask 'what-if' questions and look for hidden analogies. Artists break the rules and look at things backwards, they add something and take something away in their attempt to come up with an original idea.
- The Judge: is the role when it's time to decide if your idea is worth implementing. Judges examine if the time is right and look for things which may be wrong.
- The Warrior: is the role which carries the idea into action and does whatever is necessary to reach the objective.

The use of roles helps compartmentalize the thinking process which typically helps us to make progress, rather than giving up on an idea before it's had a proper chance for success.

The Power of Innovation

In his book, *The Power of Innovation*, Dr. Min Basadur of McMaster University, Hamilton, Ontario, Canada and founder of The Centre For Research in Applied Creativity, introduces us to a circular eight step innovation process called Simplex which cycles through four phases. Each step balances divergent thinking and each phase plays an important part in the innovation process. The Simplex innovation process is presented to us like a transforming wheel which needs to keep turning in order for the company to have a rich 'life force'.

Each of us favours a unique blend of the four Simplex phases, called our creative problem solving profile. We aren't talking about whether we are good or bad, fast or slow, but the special way in which we view problems and the strategies we employ to solve them. It's useful to know how the team is balanced to ensure that a good blend of profiles is present. The four quadrants of the innovation process are shown in Figure 11.1.

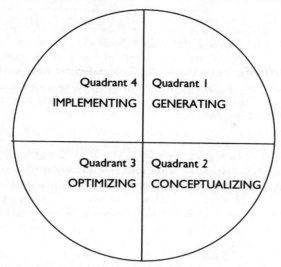

Figure 11.1 The four quadrants of the innovation process

The Basadur Simplex® Creative Problem Solving Profile

Each of us has a creative style and it's interesting to see where we map on to the innovation wheel, then compare that mapping to the role we play in the organization. The simple test as outlined in Figure 11.2 can be completed in a few minutes. To interpret the test follow the instructions in Figure 11.3 and map your score on to the grid in the same figure.

Each of us is likely to have a dominant quadrant or style and our unique blend of the four quadrants illustrates our creative problem-solving profile. We have used this test to determine if, within a team, all styles necessary to keep the wheel turning are in place. Armed with the team profiles it is interesting to post-rationalize why certain team individuals have behaved in the way they do. Why they were frustrated with other team members, and how brainstorming activities can turn into negative events with an absence of people with strong optimizing and implementing skills. Each quadrant is characterized below.

Generation

Generation involves getting the innovation process rolling. Generative thinking involves gathering information through direct experience, questioning, imagining possibilities, sensing new problems and opportunities,

This inventory is designed to describe your method of problem-solving. Give a high rank to those words which best characterize the way you problem-solve and a low rank to the words which are least characteristic of your problem-solving style You may find it hard to choose the words that best describe your problem-solving style because there are no right or wrong answers. Different characteristics described in the inventory are equally good. The aim of the inventory is to describe how you solve problems, not to evaluate your problem-solving ability.

Instructions:
Eighteen sets of four words are listed horizontally below. In each horizontal set assign a 4 to the word which best characterizes your problem-solving style, a 3 to the word which next best characterizes your problem-solving style, a 2 to the next characteristic word, and a 1 to the word which is least characteristic of you as a problem-solver. Be sure to assign a different number to each of the four words in each horizontal set. Do not make ties.

	Column 1	Column2	Column 3	Column 4
1	Alert	Poised	Ready	Eager
2	Patient	Diligent	Forceful	Prepared
3	Doing	Childlike	Detached	Realistic
4	Experiencing	Diversifying	Objective	Eliminating
5	Reserved	Serious	Fun-loving	Playful
6	Trial & Error	Alternatives	Pondering	Evaluating
7	Action	Divergence	Abstract	Convergence
8	Direct	Possibilities	Conceptual	Practicalities
9	Involved	Changing Perspectives	Theoretical	Narrowing
10	Quiet	Trustworthy	Irresponsible	Imaginative
11	Implementing	Visualizing	Modelling	Decisive
12	Hands On	Future-oriented	Reading	Detail-oriented
13	Physical	Creating Options	Thinking	Deciding
14	Impersonal	Proud	Hopeful	Fearful
15	Practicing	Transforming	Synthesizing	Choosing
16	Handling	Speculating	Fathoming	Judging
17	Sympathetic	Pragmatic	Emotional	Procrastinating
18	Contact	Novelizing	Impersonal	Making sure

Figure 11.2 Basadur creative problem-solving profile inventory

SCORING: In each column add up all the Items except Items 1, 2, 5, 10, 14 and 17 to get your column scores.

LEGEND: Column 1 scores indicate the orientation to getting knowledge for solving problems by Experiencing (direct personal involvement).
Column 2 scores indicate the orientation toward using knowledge for solving problems by Ideation (the generation of ideas without judgement).
Column 3 scores indicate the orientation toward getting knowledge for solving problems by Thinking (detached abstract theorizing).
Column 4 scores indicate the orientation toward using knowledge for solving problems by Evaluation (the application of judgement to ideas).

Post your total scores for each column on the appropriate axis below.

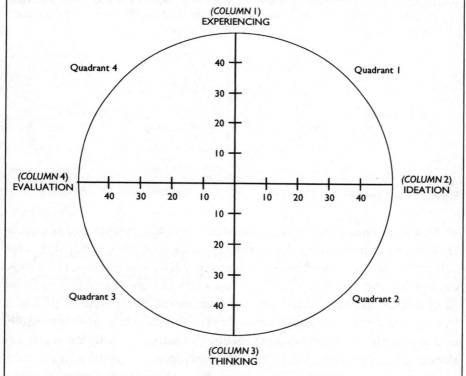

To develop your personal creative problem-solving profile, simply connect the 4 points in sequence with 4 curved lines to make a warped circle accordingly. (If you have identical column scores you will have a perfect circle. This is unlikely.) The quadrant in which your profile is most dominant indicates your strongest orientation. The other quadrants represent secondary styles accordingly. Your profile is your own unique blend of the four quadrants.

Figure 11.3 Basadur creative problem-solving profile

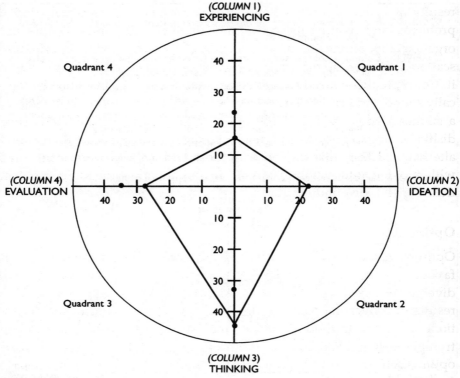

Figure 11.4 Optimizer

and viewing situations from different perspectives. People and organizations strong in generating skills prefer to come up with options, or diverge rather than evaluate and select or converge. They see relevance in almost everything and think of good and bad sides to almost any fact or issue. They dislike becoming too organized or delegating the complete problem, but are willing to let others take care of the details. They enjoy ambiguity and are hard to pin down. They delight in juggling many new projects simultaneously. Every solution they explore suggests several new problems to be solved. Thinking in this quadrant includes problem finding and fact finding.

Conceptualizing

Conceptualizing keeps the innovation process going. Like generating, it involves divergence. But rather than gaining understanding by direct experience, it favours gaining understanding by abstract thinking. It results in putting new ideas together, discovering insights that help define problems, and creating theoretical models to explain things. People and organizations strong in conceptualising skills enjoy taking information scattered all over the map from the generator phase and making sense of it. Conceptualizers need to 'understand': to them, a theory must be logically sound and precise. They prefer to proceed only with a clear grasp of a situation and when the problem or main idea is well defined. They dislike having to prioritize, implement or agonize over poorly understood alternatives. They like to play with ideas and are not overly concerned with moving into action. Thinking in this quadrant includes problem defining and idea finding.

Optimizing

Optimizing moves the innovation process further. Like conceptualizing, it favours gaining understanding by abstract thinking. But rather than diverge, an individual with this thinking style prefers to converge. This results in converting abstract ideas and alternatives into practical solutions and plans. Individuals rely on mentally testing ideas rather than on trying things out. People who favour the optimizing style prefer to create optimal solutions to a few well-defined problems or issues. They prefer to focus on specific problems and sort through large amounts of information to pinpoint 'what's wrong' in a given situation. They are usually confident in their ability to make a sound, logical evaluation and to select the best option or solution to a problem. They often lack patience with ambiguity and dislike 'dreaming' about additional ideas, points of view, or relations among problems. They believe they 'know' what the problem is. Thinking in this quadrant includes idea evaluation and selection and action planning.

Implementing

Implementing completes the innovation process. Like optimizing, it favours converging. However, it favours learning by direct experience rather than by abstract thinking. This results in getting things done. Individuals rely on trying things out rather than mentally testing them. People and organizations strong in implementing prefer situations in which they must somehow make things work. They do not need complete understanding in order to proceed and adapt quickly to changing circumstances. When a theory does not appear to fit the facts, they will readily discard it. Others perceive them as enthusiastic about getting the job done, but also impatient or even pushy as they try to turn plans and ideas into action. They will try as many different approaches as necessary and follow them as needed to ensure that the new procedure will stick. Thinking in this quadrant includes gaining acceptance and implementing.

In an organization a balance of all four is necessary to keep the innovation wheel turning. Each of the four quadrants in the creative problem solving profile is characterized by two activities:

- Generating: problem finding and fact finding
- Conceptualizing: problem definition and idea finding
- Optimizing: idea evaluation and action planning
- Implementing: gaining acceptance and implementation

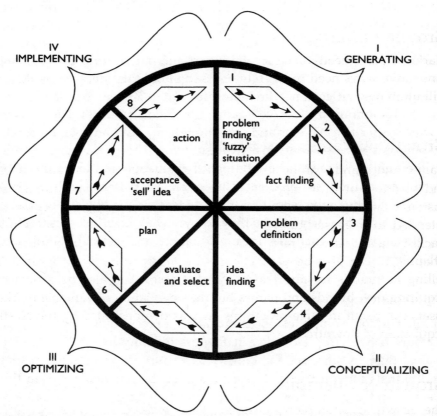

Figure 11.5 How the four quadrants correspond to the eight steps of the Simplex innovation process

---

IC Concept#34

Keep the Innovation Wheel Turning

We like this method very much, primarily because we have found that team players like to identify themselves with a particular profile and then see the value and strength of the problem solving abilities of their colleagues rather than discount them as they did before. Used together with the 'six thinking hats' method over a period of time, team members look forward to the luxury of a creative afternoon and feel very positive at the end of such meetings. This is the sort of attitude that organizations strive to create when they are considering how to add value to various intellectual capital assets.

Growth of Market Assets

Market Assets need to be constantly fed in order for them to grow. Innovative ways need to be found to add value to market assets, which will ultimately reflect a healthy business.

Growth of Names and Brands

Names and brands can be strengthened through promotion, advertising and so on. Growth in names and brands will have a direct impact on customer loyalty, repeat business and, ultimately, backlog. Campaigns intended to increase brand awareness and value should be constantly tracked via an indexing method. Methods to value brands as outlined in Chapter 12 can also be used should the organization be interested in selling its brands for any reason. Market assets can also be grown by acquiring new brands and names but the negotiation of valuable market assets can result in huge premiums, as was demonstrated by the Nestlé acquisition of Rowntree.

Growth of Champions, Customers and Evangelists

The growth of champions, customers and evangelists leads to a solid foundation from which other market assets can be grown. Customer care and satisfaction programmes will help, as will reputations for quality, responsiveness and service beyond the call of duty. Books won't tell executives how to keep customers happy or turn them into evangelists. That intelligence has to come from the market-place and surveys with customers and competitors should be regularly mounted and satisfaction indices continually monitored until they are as perfect as the organization can achieve.

Distribution, Franchise and Licensing Agreements

Many companies do not take advantage of the assets they currently own. Most don't even bother to keep an inventory of assets and their value. Alternative distribution mechanisms should be brain stormed using techniques outlined earlier in this chapter. Based on cost of sales analysis and an increasingly sophisticated and knowledgeable customer base, it may be the case that alternative, less costly distribution methods may be found. Franchise strategies have enjoyed growth in recent years. It may be that revenues can be increased by looking to see what services and products are suitable for a franchise strategy. Companies may not be keen to franchise because they like to exert greater control over their businesses than would be possible with franchisees. However faster growth can be achieved in a greater number of geographical territories than can typically be sustained with organic growth.

It Takes Nine Months to Have a Baby – No Matter How Many Women are Assigned to the Task

When the CEO wants to extend the company by increasing market assets, the normal procedure is to fire the current marketing executive and recruit one with a profile indicating they can be successful. The greatest problem with this process is that market assets are typically increased as a result in change of strategy and it is tempting to confuse the difference between strategy and tactics; and the new marketing executive is fired because anticipated results come too slow. Leaders are too quick to throw out one strategy for another, never allocating enough time for any strategy to take hold and work. This is a particularly western attitude which results in short-term planning and over-reactive management and investors. This does not appear to be a disease attributable to the Japanese who prefer to have twenty-year strategic plans. So if market assets are to be improved as a result of a new marketing direction appropriate time must be allocated to the task.

```
┌─ IC Concept#35 ──────────────────────────────────────────────┐
│                                                               │
│         IC Rich Companies Take a Long Term Perspective        │
│                                                               │
└───────────────────────────────────────────────────────────────┘
```

Growth of Intellectual Property Assets

Intellectual property assets can be expanded by research and development or by acquisition. As we have already mentioned, acquisition of intellectual property via licensing should be an option every manager of research or development should consider before embarking on proprietary R&D programmes. The business of technology brokerage is a new one and there have been some early successes. However, companies who use brokers to acquire technology to bridge an unplanned gap are usually less than enthusiastic to publicize the fact. For companies who consider themselves to be technology providers and have never planned to have an in-house distribution channel, the use of brokers is a very effective low risk revenue generating option.

Generation of Intellectual Property Assets via R&D

Research and development has long been the most popular method of generating all forms of intellectual property and in particular know-how. The major issue to consider is how to track know-how generated as a result of R&D and the trade off between patent and disclosure and trade secrets with a lesser degree of protection.

Companies that traditionally generated revenue with products where the competitive advantage was protected via patent are now re-evaluating their situation. If the provision of services is the method they use to generate revenue, then patents are less valuable than know-how. We have discussed the difficulties of identifying and recording know-how and this will be the major challenge for third millennium companies.

Growth of Infrastructure Assets

Infrastructure assets can be split into two distinct categories, those which describe management and culture and those which are a result of information technology.

Changing Management Philosophy, Processes and Culture

All companies will already have a management philosophy, processes which implement philosophy and a corporate culture. So it's inappropriate to consider 'growing' them as it's more likely they will require to be changed.

Changing management philosophy and processes is the subject of hundreds of business books. Examples include re-engineering, *kaizen* and TQM. Changing philosophy may be the only way in which a company can achieve its goals and such changes typically take a while and are associated with initial costs.

To change a corporate culture takes time and is expensive. In their book on the subject Deal and Kennedy have estimated that to change a corporate culture a company must spend between five and ten percent of its average budget for the personnel whose behaviour is supposed to be changed. For a large organization that's millions of dollars a year. If the organization has a particularly strong culture it may also take years to change. A better decision may be to shut it down and start over. It's a sort of 'no pain no gain' situation. The sooner the transition is over the better.

Creating IT Infrastructures

Information technology systems should be designed and built to support corporate functions. Custom systems will of course need to be built and may be costly. Networking systems such as e-mail and the World Wide Web are very inexpensive and can have a huge impact on communications infrastructure overnight.

IT managers in the third millennium enterprise are certainly key figures as it is their role to plan and grow IT infrastructure. How long the plan extends into the future will depend on the criticality of the system. Where

IT systems form the heart of the enterprise such as those for the airline industry we anticipate plans will have a twenty-year plus outlook.

```
┌─ IC Concept#36 ─────────────────────────────────────────┐
│                                                          │
│        Grow Intellectual Capital for Tomorrow's Needs    │
│                                                          │
└──────────────────────────────────────────────────────────┘
```

Growth of Human-centred Assets

People can be developed in a variety of ways, education, training, via job experience and through the process of being alive. From the perspective of the individual their growth is essential if they wish to be employed for the rest of their life and continual investment in growth should be a high priority. Education is still considered to be a privilege by many and perhaps that's because time off to attend class and payment of fees is definitely a bonus. Perhaps a better way would be to give every employee a number of 'sabbatical days', say five to ten each year, which they would apply to their manager to use in a number of ways. Attendance of training courses and conferences, or writing an article or paper for a journal would all be valid reasons to use the days, it's up to the individual and the manager to decide how to spend the time. The key is to use the days to mutual benefit. Payment for education is always an issue; some prefer to pay only when a success factor is established, such as passing an exam or the publication of a paper.

Growth via Education

As children we were always told that a good education was a valuable thing. Most of us didn't pay any attention. The ability to communicate with colleagues in all ways is a part of contributing towards the wealth of the organization so employers should be discussing education opportunities with their staff. It is particularly important to be able to write clearly which many could improve. Also the ability to analyse a problem and decompose its constituent parts – a natural skill for some, but a process which can be learned by others. These are vital abilities if the organization is to derive maximum benefit from knowledge rich employees.

Occupational Assessments

Occupational assessments help both employee and employer to decide what type of growth opportunity is appropriate for each individual.

Again, we stress the use of as wide a range of such tests as possible to broaden the possibilities for the individual, not limit them.

Vocational Qualifications

Vocational qualifications are a good source of enrichment for employees and organizations should consider the costs of developing and keeping a knowledge rich work-force versus the risks associated with staff turnover to acquire new skills. There is a general reticence by some organizations to use modern technology, such as e-mail and the World Wide Web, primarily because they are frightened of it. Imagine deciding not to use the phone because of a lack of knowledge of digital switching systems. An attitude in the organization where representatives were always on top of innovations in business practice, is a must for third millennium enterprises and the promotion of vocational qualifications is one way of achieving that.

Work Related Knowledge and Competencies

Work related knowledge and competencies are built up over time by performing and excelling in one job after another. Large companies occasionally have policies where a significant proportion of their work-force change jobs every three years. It is interesting to note how employees of companies with this policy appear 'new to the job' and attack new problems with the enthusiasm typically ascribed to newcomers.

One problem with the generation of job related knowledge and competencies is that the employee becomes valuable not only to the employer but also to the competition, so the challenge is how to balance growth of knowledge and competencies with risk management. One method, of course, is to try to capture such valuable assets so they are not attributable to just a small number within the organization.

Training

Training is another way of disseminating knowledge owned by the few to the many. However, we promote more knowledge sharing by those within the company via informal training sessions. One high technology organization used to hold an internal Friday seminar for the corporate technical community which would be posted within the company. Volunteers would talk about their project, research whatever to an average audience of ten. The new marketing director, a function traditionally scorned by the technical community, had failed to get a meeting to meet the VP of R&D or any key technical personnel in the company. So he volunteered to give a presentation to the seminar group entitled: 'How I'm designing the marketing strategy'. When the day came, the director was surprised to discover that the presentation would be in the auditorium to an audience of eighty! Every technical person in the company was there, including the Vice President of R&D, and quizzed him in great detail for three and a half hours. Mission accomplished.

Research and Development

Research and development is a primary way of developing knowledge-able employees. The challenge is in separating the knowledge from the human and disseminating it to colleagues who could benefit from it. The relationship between research and development and corporate strategy should be examined to ensure that development of intellectual property including know-how, contributes towards corporate goals.

Monitoring Growth of Intellectual Capital

Growth of intellectual capital can be managed if a series of projects of tasks is designed and monitored against performance goals such as indices. In Figure 11.6 each of the bars represents a project designed to generate intellectual capital. For example, Project A could be an R&D project to generate some know-how, project E to improve customer loyalty and so on. We specifically recommend starting projects whose sole aim is to increase the quality and value of intellectual capital for its own sake and not just as a spin-off of some other activity.

┌─ IC Concept#37 ───┐

The Ability to Collaborate is an Asset

└──┘

Growth via Collaboration

The ability to successfully collaborate for the growth of any type of asset is actually an infrastructure asset which is derived from corporate culture, management philosophy and processes. Where there is a match between

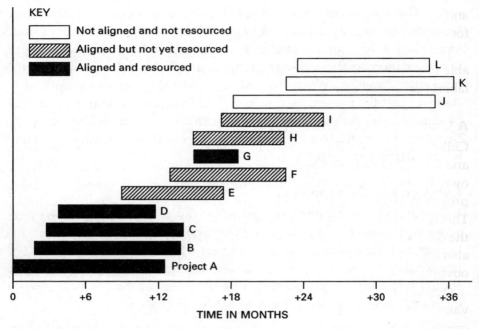

Figure 11.6 Monitoring the growth of intellectual capital

two or more companies and the project is suitable for collaboration, all partners can achieve significant benefits. On average, collaborations between companies do not tend to last more than four years. Our research has shown that collaborations that do not make it are typically terminated due to a mismatch of corporate cultures. The second greatest reason for the failure of collaborations is the lack of quality of market research prior to the commencement of the collaboration. This eventuality means that there was already a product on the market or that the collaboration proved pointless and its results were pre-empted in the market by a competitor. These two reasons can both be attributed to misunderstanding intellectual capital. In the first case, the partners did not take the time to determine that their cultures would enable them to work together. In the second case, neither partner had a clear understanding of its potential market assets.

A Big Bet

In order to be successful, collaborations must be a 'big bet'. This means that both partners must have a lot to win if the collaboration is a success, and a lot to lose if it fails. Where one partner takes the major risk, the basis for collaboration is weakened.

The goal of the collaboration should be clear and all parties must be able to subscribe to it. Again, where one party has a secret agenda the collaboration is weakened.

A Culture of Their Own

Collaborations which pull together a team from more than one company and last for more than a few months also tend to develop a culture of their own. It should mirror the nature of the task in hand and the values of the project management. It might inherit rights and rituals from its 'parents'. This is good because the culture of the team binds it together and gives it the cohesion it will need to be successful. However, that same culture will also fight off attempts to stop or close down the collaboration, even if it is obviously a failure.

Over a period of time the goal of the collaboration may change, or even vanish altogether. In order to ensure that collaborations don't just continue because they have a momentum of their own, they should be regularly evaluated. The Collaboration Performance Evaluator – a self-test questionnaire set out below – forms the basis for regular monitoring of business collaborations.

The Collaboration Performance Evaluator

- Who is the company champion for the project?
- What are the top 3 goals that the collaboration has to achieve within the next _____ months?
- Will the collaboration achieve these goals?
- What would make the collaboration a greater success?
- Has the financial plan for the collaboration been completed?
- How is the collaboration performing with respect to the plan? (Revenues & costs as a % of plan)
- What are the reasons for the divergence from plan?
- Is any action planned to get the collaboration back on track?
- What actions?
- Has dissolving the project been considered?
- If 'no', why not?

Management
- What are the resources for managing this collaboration?
- Board Members
- Steering Committee
- Management Team
- Integration Manager
- Management Team
- Collaboration Manager

Cultural Issues
- Who is the leader for this collaboration?
- Is there more than one leader?
- Who are the managers within this collaboration?
- How would you describe the culture of your collaborator?
- In what major ways does the culture of your collaborator differ from yours?
- Are there any elements of the collaboration that you consider to be risky due to the difference in corporate cultures?
- Are the activities of the collaboration split across several geographic locations?
- If 'yes', what provisions have been made to ensure that all activities are appropriately co-ordinated?

Technical Issues
- List the technical goals for this collaboration
- Have sufficient resources been allocated to ensure the technical success of this project?
- Management
- Technical Leadership
- Hardware/Software Resources
- Is the time schedule realistic?
- Is the project infrastructure appropriate for this collaboration?

Risk Analysis
- What are the major risks to this project which may result in failure to meet plan?
- List the containment/ back up plans for each identified risk

Ranking

- Rank the progress of the collaboration (out of 10) with respect to the following elements
- Ability of the partners to perform
- Technical qualification of the team
- Project management
- Competitive issues
- Ability to stick to schedule
- Compatibility of corporate cultures
- Market research
- Positioning the relationship in the market
- Generation and protection of intellectual property
- Legal structure of the project   Total

Collaborative Project Self-Test Questionnaire

1   General Questions

- Has the business relationship between the collaborators been documented?
- What will be the duration of the collaboration?
- Is it realistic to enter into this collaboration for this time period?
- Have you ever worked with any of the collaborators before?
- Under what circumstances will the collaboration be dissolved?
- What are the major benefits of the collaboration to you?
- What are the major benefits of the collaboration to the other partners?
- What are the major risk factors in this collaboration?
- How can those risks be contained?
- List the major risks for each of the partners together with ways in which those risks might be contained.
- Are there any outside agencies involved in this collaboration?
- In what ways could those agencies contribute towards risk?

2   Legal Structure of the Collaboration

- What is the legal structure of the collaboration?
- Who is responsible for authorizing the 'legality' of the collaboration?

- Has the legal agreement been put in place before the collaboration begins?
- Do you understand every word in this agreement?
- Has the legal agreement been signed by all parties?
- Does the legal agreement reflect the original reason for the collaboration?
- Are there any subcontractors?
- Who is responsible for managing the subcontractors?
- Do the subcontractors have a contract, work schedule and so on?
- Have any verbal agreements been made between collaborators?
- Who will document those agreements?
- Is the contract for goods, services or know-how?
- Have you sent letters of intent or heads of agreement?
- What is the reason for sending the above instead of a contract?
- Have any guarantees been given?
- Are the impact of these understood?
- Are you in a position of ownership to satisfy all aspects of the contract into which you have entered?
- Have issues of breach, indemnity and negligence been given consideration?
- Under which law and jurisdiction is this contract agreed?
- Is this a balanced contract?
- How much will it cost to operate this contract?

3   **Intellectual Property**
- Will this contract generate any new IP?
- What will be the nature if the new IP?
- Has ownership of background rights been made clear before commencing the contract?
- Has ownership of new IP (foreground rights) been agreed?
- List ownership of foreground rights.
- Is there joint ownership of any IP?
- If 'yes', why?
- List all the situations where deadlock can occur.
- Is there any risk of your IP rights jeopardizing potential business scenarios?

4 The Collaboration Agreement

- Has the Collaboration Agreement been specifically designed for this collaboration?
- Have all partners signed it?
- Are there any interested third parties who need to see this Agreement?
- Does the Agreement reflect the business need for the partners?
- Has a mechanism been put in place to update the Collaboration Agreement over the duration of the contract?
- Do you understand every word of the Collaboration Agreement?

5 Impact of Corporate Culture

- Have you undertaken a culture audit to see how the partners fit together?
- Have you identified the major areas where differing corporate cultures may present a risk to the project?
- What measures have you put in place to minimize the impact of differing corporate cultures?
- Is there any risk to intellectual property caused by corporate culture clash?
- Could culture clash cause any quality problems?

6 Commercial Framework

- Describe the commercial framework for this collaboration.
- Referring to 'What are the major benefits of the collaboration to the other partners?' (Section 1) check that the chosen commercial framework reflects the benefits to the partners.
- Undertake the same analysis referring to the risks each partner has to manage.
- How will the correctness of finances between partners be checked over the period of the collaboration?

12

Valuing Intellectual Capital

We have taken a lot of time to discuss why it's important to understand the value of intellectual capital within the organization. In this chapter we will discuss the issue of valuing it in the accounting sense. In their discussion paper on Goodwill and Intangible Assets, published in 1994, The UK Accounting Standards Board notes that in a survey of 370 acquisitions, it was found that the amount paid for purchased goodwill, as a percentage of the acquirers' net worth pre-acquisition, grew from 1 percent in 1976 to 44 per cent in 1987. This fact supports our premise that there has been a substantial shift in the way companies are perceived as valuable. The market clearly believes there is more to a company than the tangible assets. The problem is that goodwill tends to be treated as a 'catch all' so even though it's possible to say that the intangible assets of the company have value, there isn't usually an itemized list. There are exceptions, notably brands and high profile patents, but it's not necessary to own the patent for the ring-pull can to have something of value.

What Do Investors Do?

Investors have always valued intellectual capital. When a venture capitalist is looking to invest in a seed or start-up venture, there is usually nothing tangible to invest in at all. So what do they look at and how do they make decisions? These days venture capitalists look at people, people and people, then the idea and the market. They are trying to assess the 'pull it off factor' of a specific team of individuals. It's hard to get more intangible than that. But some venture capitalists do make a high return on investment. When an investor is investing in a going concern, or perhaps acquiring it, what do they do? They will look at the quality of R&D, the life of intellectual property, the quality of the management team. They will examine existing computer systems which provide infrastructure and see if they fulfil their function, are modern and based on standards. They will look to see if they are extensible. They will look at the corporate beliefs and culture and try to determine if any plans for merging will succeed – will the two cultures be able to merge? If they're really switched on they will also interview key customers and wander about the company looking for employee morale and staff loyalty to the company and its management team. Then based on all this information, a wealth of financial data and on tangible assets they will make their decision.

IC Concept#38

Not all that's Valuable is Tangible

Why Value Intellectual Capital?

So intellectual capital has been valued for years, but only when it's necessary for the purposes of sale. Just because a significant proportion of corporate assets are intangible doesn't mean they should not be valued. Several reasons for valuing intellectual capital include:

- To enable managers to understand where value lies in the company
- To have a metric for assessing success and growth
- As the basis for raising finance or loans

Cash is a universal currency. If a company's cash value is increasing it becomes more valuable. Obvious of course, but then why don't companies value intangible assets as a matter of course. Two reasons:

1 They don't have to
2 There are no agreed methods

Each year companies are required to report on the status of their business, to their shareholders and to the government. Indeed, there are two categories of assets on the balance sheet which could be used to represent parts of intellectual capital value: goodwill and intangible assets. However, the guidelines for treatment of these two categories pre-dates the time when 44% of a company's net worth was intangible. It is not fashionable to produce balance sheets with that bias. But things are changing. The very existence of software companies is challenging some of these ideas.

Intangible Assets, Goodwill and Intellectual Capital

To some extent the concept of developing valuable intellectual capital is at odds with accounting methods traditionally used for intangible assets and goodwill. When a company pays an amount to acquire another company and a portion of that amount is ascribed to goodwill and intangible assets, traditionally the cost of both is either written off against reserves or depreciated over an amount of time, which varies from country to country. This reflects a philosophy that the intangible assets and goodwill will lose their value over a period of time. In modern times, the trend is reversed and intangible assets, in particular the value of brands and trade marks, are increasing in value not decreasing. Some brands outlive time periods legislated for their depreciation and are considerably more valuable than before. This is a reflection of the global economy and the use of global media campaigns which develop and strengthen brands and therefore the companies that own them. Other aspects of goodwill which are traditionally depreciated over time are the royalties which are derived from licensing patents. That procedure makes sense, as eventually the patent will expire and royalties cease. But know-how stays with the company as long as the employee stays and there is no mechanism for putting a value on the know-how of the work-force. The system needs to be reviewed to reflect the requirements of third millennium companies. After all, the double-entry bookkeeping system is over five hundred years old. Times have changed.

Putting Intangible Assets on the Balance Sheet

Should we be putting intellectual capital on the balance sheet? Is intellectual capital the competitive advantage we should keep secret? There are aspects of intellectual capital which in our opinion should definitely go on the balance sheet for all to see, brands already appear, as do royalties. Computer software should appear when it is an evolving product. The contents of goodwill should be 'opened' and renamed to reflect modern requirements. We believe it should cease to be treated as a 'catch all', as it will ultimately become disproportionately large. Then it will be odd to have half the accounts categorized and accurate to the last bean and the other half lumped into one category and valued by ad hoc methods driven by market forces.

If You've Got it Flaunt it – The Skandia Solution

Skandia AFS perceived their intellectual capital as a huge hidden asset and in 1993, led by Leif Edvinsson, published their first balanced annual report on intellectual capital. The document, which is publicly available with the numbers removed, was a highly innovative step for Skandia to take. We quote from their material:

> The intellectual capital in Skandia AFS means – among other things – our possession of knowledge, applied experience, organizational technology, customer relationships, professional skills and intercultural skills within the entire organization – the collective knowledge embedded in human capital and structural capital that gives Skandia AFS a competitive edge on the market. The value of intellectual capital is determined by the extent to which these intangible assets will be turned into financial returns for AFS as a whole. The goal of the IC Function is the growth and development of intellectual capital as visible, lasting value complimentary to the traditional balance sheet. In a very real sense, the ultimate aim is to convert IQ into ECU.
>
> *Skandia AFS*

In 1994 Skandia published its second intellectual capital report, a twenty-two page colour, glossy brochure which explained the rationale behind the report and some measures and indicators for intellectual capital which is of value to Skandia. Categories include: Finance, Customer, Process and Renewal and Development Focus. It's an interesting document which when read by Skandia customers will no doubt reassure them that Skandia is investing in the long haul. As they are a financial services company, that reassurance will have an impact on repeat business, cancellation of policies and so on.

Skandia's decision to share information concerning their intangible assets looks like it is paying off. Leif Edvinsson has spent a lot of time and energy merchandising the Skandia message. His photograph has even been on the cover of *Fortune* magazine.

The Special Significance of Software Companies

The need to consider the financial value of intellectual capital is clearly demonstrated by software companies. The only assets a software company needs are a few computers, desks, chairs and phones. They don't need to be together in one place all the time as they can communicate and send code to each other over the Internet. They can talk over the phone and meet in hotel lobbies with their prospective customers. They can distribute products electronically, software, manuals the lot. They can provide customer support over the phone and on the Internet. Finally, they can demonstrate their wares in a World Wide Web shop-front. The tangible assets of such a company with six employees would be less than $35,000 – hardly worth the effort of hiring an accountant. But their sales could be millions. Many software companies start this way. Their product, software, is as intangible as its copyright. Once it's on the market value can be ascribed using sales projections, but whilst it's being built there is no agreed method of valuing it. This is currently a hot topic and because of the volume and massive value of computer software we anticipate there will be an agreed international method of valuing software within the next decade.

Assessing the value of IC is dependent upon the goals of the organization and the state of the market. An automatic valuation scheme needs to be designed for each organization, based on what IC is important to them at any point in time.

Who Values Intellectual Capital?

At the time of writing no one purports to value intellectual capital as a service other than The Technology Broker.

Valuation Makes Things Valuable

Valuing Assets

Methods for valuing assets include cost based, market based, and the income approach, each of which is described below.

The Cost Approach

The cost approach is utilized to arrive at the value of the asset by ascertaining its replacement cost. The assumption underlying this approach is that price of the new asset is commensurate with the economic value of the service that the new asset can provide during its life. The principle disadvantage of this method lies in its correlation of cost with value. This is a particular problem in technological areas. A commonly cited example is the US Government's attempt to build a nuclear-powered aircraft in the 1950s. The costs of this ultimately abortive project will have amounted to many millions of dollars, yet the value of the aircraft, which wouldn't fly, was zero.

Even in cases where the cost of replacement might reasonably be expected to provide value there is an additional complication. The appraiser or valuer has to quantify the necessary reduction from the brand new state of the replacement asset to the actual state of the asset under consideration, taking into account the physical, functional, economic and legal life of the asset.

Market Approach

The market approach arrives at the value of an asset by obtaining a consensus of what others in the market-place have judged it to be. Problems here include the requirement for an active and public market, with a record of exchange of comparable properties.

The Income Approach

The income approach looks at the income producing capability of the property to be valued. The future economic benefits are equated to the present value of the net cash flows anticipated to be derived from ownership of the property. The quantification of the future cash flows should take into account incremental fixed assets and working capital investments.

The calculation of the present value of the cash flows is arrived at by utilizing an appropriate discount value of the factor. This factor can be derived from a rate of returns model, each company will have its own favourite.

Valuing Market Assets

Some market assets have been valued for a long time. Notable examples include trade marks and brands. Those interested in valuing trade marks and brands may wish to hire the services of a brand valuation expert. One published method for valuing brands is based on scoring seven factors which are attributed to the brand:

- Leadership
- Stability
- Market
- Internationality
- Trend
- Support
- Protection

The value of the brand increases with its strength, which can be determined from analysis of income flows. The brand's strength increases gradually over time until it moves into the number two or weak number one position when there is an exponential effect on its value.

Valuing Repeat Business, Backlog and Customer Loyalty

The financial value of customer loyalty is actually measured by repeat business and that is determined via sales projections. Valuing via any projections is risky as none of us can predict eventualities such as war. For example, the Gulf war had a drastic impact on business travel, especially international business travel, as many perceived the airlines of those countries which joined together to fight Iraq to be prime guerrilla targets.

Most companies are able to project revenues a year ahead, but predicting accurately any longer than that lacks credibility for the accounting profession. Valuing backlog is easier as the orders are already received, yet the asset isn't tangible until the cash is in the bank!

Most market assets are not too difficult to value using one or all of the three methods outlined above and we are used to thinking about assets close to the market in monetary terms – that's why they're called market assets.

Valuing Intellectual Property Assets

When valuing intellectual property a primary consideration is the strength of protection. One aspect is the strength and generic nature of the claims which gives the owner of the patent a wide spectrum of applications in which a monopoly is held. Another dimension is the geographic territory in which the owner's patent is filed. However, a world-wide patent with wide ranging claims may be of little value if there is no market pull for industrial applications which require it. The life expectancy of a patent will also determine its value, a newly granted patent with twenty years' protection will be more valuable than one which has only a year to go before the patent lapses. Patents can be valued because of the revenue they can generate for the owner who can receive royalties or because of the value the owner has in stopping a competitor from using them. In the former case, value can be ascertained using one of the methods already mentioned. In the latter, the value of the market share enjoyed by the owner which is displaced from the competition would have to be estimated.

Valuing Infrastructure Assets

Valuing infrastructure assets is a bit trickier, yet aspects of that are done every day too. When a company makes an acquisition of a going concern they are buying a business complete with all its assets. They might, however, consider that with a different management team the business would be more valuable. This is the basis for venture capital investment in management buy-outs. Rule of thumb valuations may say that a business was worth last or next year's sales, if you were an optimist. So the value of infrastructure comes bundled with the rest. The acquisition may be perceived as one unit which generates value. On the other hand, the true value of the enterprise might just be its infrastructure assets; for example, its corporate culture might be perceived as valuable because it was sympathetic to another the purchaser proposed to merge it with. Acquisitions which look very attractive don't always occur, primarily because the acquirers thought that cultures would not merge.

Valuing the Impact of Infrastructure

Most companies rely on information technology to some extent. It's clear that some organizations, such as banks, could never offer the range of services they do without IT solutions, most of which are custom built. Suppliers of IT solutions have developed cost benefit analysis methods to help convince customers to decide to invest in IT solutions. Where IT infrastructure enables a new service to be introduced then its value added can be calculated using either the cost or income approach.

When a system is being replaced and perhaps integrated with another in order to gain benefits throughout a company, additional benefits should be analysed in order to determine if the added value of integration is worth the investment. For example, if a crew scheduling system for an airline which operated independently was replaced by one which integrated with production planning, catering and inventory, the added value would need to be clearly quantified before its benefits could be analysed. The IC auditor would then need to be able to determine the difference between added functionality that 'was nice' from that which 'was of value'. That would require a survey of all types of prospective users of the system in order to identify and measure the benefit. Then one of the valuation methods can be chosen.

Valuing Human-centred Assets

The traditional way to show value for people is by their salary. Valuable people get paid more than those who are less so. Unique individuals are typically valuable and are therefore paid more too. But that's a very superficial way of looking at the value of people. As we have already stated, people are typically under-utilized in the company, they have talents and value that may not be reflected in their salary because they are not providing that value. In order to see employees in their true perspective it's first necessary to put them in their optimal job, then look at the role they play in the company. The next step is to see what other intangible benefits they have, such as knowledge, team leadership, creative ability and so on and put a value on that too. This is a non trivial on-going process. A lack of knowledge in the organization at the right place at the right time, costs money. It costs money if the organization has to reinvent technology, or even if someone spends an hour figuring out how to send a purchase order. In order to determine what knowledge is of value and who needs to use it, the process of building even a rudimentary paper knowledge base has to be attempted. Once it's known who needs and uses what knowledge the valuation process can slowly begin.

Is Your Message Valuable For Me?

Sometimes a piece of information arrives unexpectedly and it starts a chain reaction. A casual conversation reveals a hidden gem, which solves a problem, or even starts a whole new idea flowing. This is most easily observed by watching researchers – as they read and share their ideas with others they are able to solve each other's problems.

Fermat's Last Theorem – Messages from over Three Hundred Years

At the age of ten whilst browsing through his public library, Andrew Wiles stumbled across the world's greatest mathematical puzzle. Fermat's Last Theorem, which had baffled mathematicians for over 300 years. But from that day, little Andrew dreamed of solving it.

Pythagoras's Theorem for right-angled triangles is the simplest of mathematical equations: $x^2 + y^2 = z^2$. However, in 1637, a French mathematician, Pierre de Fermat said that this equation could not be true for $x^3 + y^3 = z^3$ or for any equation $x^n + y^n = z^n$ where n is greater than 2. Tantalisingly, he wrote on his Greek text: 'I have discovered a truly marvellous proof, which this margin is too narrow to contain.' No one had found the proof and for 350 years attempts to prove 'FLT' attracted huge prizes, mistaken and eccentric claims and met with failure.

In 1986, an extraordinary idea linked this irritating problem with one of the most profound ideas of modern mathematics: the Taniyama-Shimura Conjecture, named after a young Japanese mathematician who tragically committed suicide. The link meant that if Taniyama was true then so must be FLT.

For seven years, Wiles worked in his attic study at Princeton, telling no one but his family. In June 1993 he reached his goal. At a three-day lecture at Cambridge, he outlined a proof of Taniyama – and with it Fermat's Last Theorem.

Then disaster struck. His colleague, Dr Nick Katz, made a tiny request for clarification. It turned into a gaping hole in the proof. So Andrew Wiles retired back to his attic. He shut out everything, but Fermat.

A year later, at the point of defeat, he had a revelation. Returning to first principles he decided to go back and look one more time at the hole in the proof to try and pinpoint exactly why it wasn't working. Suddenly he realized that what was holding him up was exactly what would resolve this problem and one he'd had in an attempt on another theory, Iwasawa, three years earlier. The very flaw was the key to a strategy he had abandoned years before. In an instant Fermat was proved.

One of the great things about this work is it embraces the ideas of so many mathematicians. A partial list would include: Klein, Fricke, Hurwitz, Hecke, Dirichlet, Dedekind, the proof by Langlands and Tunnell, Deligne, Rapoport, Katz, Mazur's idea of using the deformation theory of Galois representations, Igusa, Eichler, Shimura, Taniyama, Frey's reduction, Bloch, Kato, Selmer, Frey, and Fermat. The message has to be in the right place before it has value.

Technology Pushes – But Only if You Know That It Exists

In the early days of technology broking we thought we'd ring around the major computer manufacturers and ask them what technology they thought they would need in, say, a one or two year timeframe. Instead of giving us their shopping list, they said 'What have you got?'. Cynics would say that's because they didn't want to tell us their strategy, we think not. They knew exactly what they wanted to do , but hadn't decided exactly how. They're technology driven. So this type of information or technology is only valuable when it's in the right place at the right time. It's serendipity. Pooling knowledge bites and creating corporate memory is one way in which we can begin to bring some control to the problem.

VCs Invest in People

Rule of thumb valuations may say that a business is worth last years or, if you were an optimist, next year's sales. In that case, key assets which are essential for the continued success of the business would need to be identified. Some of these would no doubt be people and so their continued presence is valued and that value may be reflected in more favourable employment contracts.

When a venture capitalist invests in a seed business he is investing in people and an idea. So the initial capitalization of a business can be seen as the value of the individuals in the team.

Valuing Intellectual Capital – The Way Forward

The intangible assets of a company are clearly not homogeneous, so it is silly to assume that one method will work for all assets. It's also easier to value some assets such as trade marks and patents than the impact of IT or the potential of knowledge. There are so many variables to consider. But the IC auditor should not be daunted. Pick something easy to start, then progress to more difficult challenges. There are several organizations that have decided to take up the gauntlet and value their intellectual capital. Over the next couple of years the critical mass of those with expertise will grow. Watch this space.

Intellectual Capital Valuation Questions
- What is the major reason for valuing your intellectual capital?
- What valuation methods will you use for:
  - market assets?
  - human-centred assets?
  - infrastructure assets?
  - intellectual property assets?
- To whom will you communicate this information?
- How will you feed this back into your corporate planning system?

Last Words

We have discussed the process of identifying, documenting, auditing and recording intellectual capital. Our method brings together intangible assets which most companies already have but fail to manage in a coherent way. There is still much to do and learn from research. In particular, we need to know more about corporate knowledge management and the creation of corporate memories. Organizations that realize their ability to succeed in the third millennium will be dominated by intangible assets are already putting their intellectual capital teams together.

The intellectual capital audit forms the basis of the corporate health check for the third millennium enterprise.

IC Concept#40

The Future is Intangible

Summary of IC Concepts

#1   – Enterprise = Tangible Assets + Intellectual Capital
#2   – Intellectual Capital Sharpens the Cutting Edge
3   – Brands Outlive Companies
4   – Cherish Loyal Customers
5   – Position Distribution as an Asset
6   – Patents Protect Profits
7   – Intellectual Property is a Corporate Investment
8   – Valuable Employers and Employees Invest in Themselves
9   – Knowledge Rich Employees Add Value
10 – Protect and Grow Core Competencies
11 – Manage Human Resources
12 – Match Management Philosophy to Market Needs
13 – Make Corporate Culture an Asset
#14 – Collaborate for Greater Achievements
#15 – IT Infrastructure is Corporate Backbone
#16 – Identify Goals, Audit Intangibles, Assess Strength
#17 – Auditing Intellectual Capital Needs Multidisciplinary Teams

#18 – Measurement Identifies Assets
#19 – Know What Optimal Looks Like
#20 – Validate the Market – Measure Market Assets
#21 – Protect the Future – Measure Intellectual Property Assets
#22 – Get the Right Tools – Measure Infrastructure Assets
#23 – Grow People Power – Measure Human-centred Assets
#24 – Management Needs Measurement
#25 – IC Index = Corporate Health Indicator
#26 – Constantly Track Intellectual Capital
#27 – Intellectual Capital = Corporate Sustainability
#28 – Differentiate Through Intangibles
#29 – IC Management is a Continual Process
#30 – Put Knowledge Into Every Process
#31 – Know About Your Corporate Knowledge
#32 – Build a Corporate Memory
#33 – Knowledge means Power and Profits
#34 – Keep the Innovation Wheel Turning
#35 – IC Rich Companies Take a Long Term Perspective
#36 – Grow Intellectual Capital for Tomorrow's Needs
#37 – The Ability to Collaborate is an Asset
#38 – Not all that's Valuable is Tangible
#39 – Valuation Makes Things Valuable
#40 – The Future is Intangible

Glossary

Aspect an attribute of an asset

Asset an intangible with the potential to contribute value

Asset ranking organization of assets according to pre and post conditions

Backlog orders in process for goods and services

Behaviour how an asset behaves depending upon actions which prevail upon it

Brand the combined position, image, symbol, name or design intended to identify goods or services from those of competitors

Brand Identity the position and perception of the brand in the market place

Brand Loyalty the extent to which customers continue to buy a brand in preference to any other

Brand Positioning the message created by a brand in the mind of a prospective customer

Brand Strategy the method which an organization adopts in order to take a desired position in the market-place

Class a set of assets which share a common function

Collaboration where several assets combine to achieve a desired effect

Constraints the limiting factors which determine the methods which can be used on an asset

Coupling the interdependence between aspects

Champion an individual within a customer organization who acts as a catalyst for sales of an external organization's products and services

Confidentiality Agreement same as trade secret agreement

Copyright an ownership right granted to an author of a written work ownership rights on written word

Customer an individual or organization who has purchased goods and services

Design Right right preventing others from copying an original design

Distribution Channels the mechanism a company uses to sell its goods and services to its customers

Domain the 'world' in which we are viewing the asset

Evangelist an individual within a customer organization who actively promotes an external organizations' products and services and also acts as a Champion

Exploitation the extent to which an asset is optimized in the market-place

Favoured Contracts contracts existing giving the organization a favourable position, typically generated due to a strength of bargaining power on the part of the organization

Franchise a contract between a franchisor and a franchisee which enables the franchisee to exploit a name, process or equipment and the goodwill and know-how associated with it in return for a consideration

High Values the optimal state for a particular aspect of an asset

IC Index the ranking of aspects and assets based on their percentage achievement of high values

IC Knowledge Base the place where all knowledge and information concerning an asset is kept

Infringement unlawful violation of intellectual property

Know-how knowledge owned by an individual

License permission granted by an owner of intellectual property granting certain rights to another

Licensing rights owned by a company to manufacture, market or sell goods and services originating from another enterprise

Method process whereby some aspect of an asset is measured and valued

Non- Disclosure Agreement same as trade secret agreement

Optimal Asset Set the optimal set of assets to achieve a stated goal

Patent a monopoly right, which is property, which can be bought, sold, hired, or licensed

Position the message which comes into the mind of the prospect when they hear a company, product or brand name

Post condition status of assets after application of a method

Precondition essential status of assets prior to application of a method

Process Diagrams show the steps which comprise a method

Prospect a profiled individual who has the perceived requirements to buy goods and services

Registered Designs protects novel designs with eye appeal

Repeat Business where the customer is expected to return to the same supplier of goods and services

Service Mark a mark or sign which is capable of being represented graphically and which distinguishes services of one company from another

Status the measurement of an asset according to the method used

Strategic Alliances relationships with other companies or organizations in order to gain a favourable position in the market-place or leverage joint resources to mutual benefit

Suspect an individual who has characteristics which identify them as a prospective customer

Trade Mark a mark or sign which is capable of being represented graphically and which distinguishes goods of one company from another

Trade Secret an industrial secret normally protected by an agreement

Transition the process of moving from one state to another

Viewpoint a set of assets and their relevant aspects

REFERENCES AND FURTHER READING

Aaronson, J. (1995) Eyeball to Eyeball with China, *Business Week*, Feb 20.

Abell, M. (1990) *The International Franchise Option*, Waterlow.

Adams, D. (1979) *The Hitch Hikers Guide to the Galaxy*, Pan Books.

Anderson, A. and Bertelotti, N. (1995) Valuing Intellectual Property. *Managing Intellectual Property*, February.

ASE (1995) ASE Psychometric Tests and Software.

ASE (1995) ASE Training.

Bannister, N. (1995) BT Ordered to foot lion's share of bill for number portability. *The Guardian*, December 15.

Bannock, G. and Peacock, A. (1992) *Takeovers And Industrial Policy – A Defence*, The David Hume Institute.

Bao, T. (1995) IP Law Aspects in Strategic Planning. *Mananging Intellectual Property*, March.

Barnes, W. (1995) Leading for Results. *Executive Excellence*, March 8.

Basadur, Dr M. (1994) *Simplex A Flight to Creativity*, The Creative Education Foundation.

Basadur, Dr M. (1986) *The Power of Innovation*, Pitman.

Bernold, T. (1986) *Expert Systems and Knowledge Engineering*, Elsevier Science Publishers.

Birkin, M. (1993) How to get a grip on the great untouchables. *Financial Director*, October.

Black, T. (1989) *Intellectual Property In Industry*, Butterworth.

Block, P. (1987) *The Empowered Manager*, Jossey-Bass.

Booch, G. (1994) *Object-Oriented Analysis and Design*, Benjamin/Cummings Publishing.

Braiman, L. K. (1995) Hot Growth Companies. *Business Week*, May 22.

British Psychological Society (1992) *Psychological Testing – A Guide*, March.

Brown, M. and Laverick, S. (1994) *Measuring Corporate Performance*, Pergamon.

Bucci, A. (1994) Managing. *Business Week*, October 31.

Campbell, A. and Verbeke, A. (1994) *The Globalization of Service Multinationals*, Pergamon.

Charles, F. (1993) The Virtual Corporation. *Business Week*, Feb 8.

Chu, F. (1994) Investment Returns and Capital Mobility. *The Bankers Magazine*, May–June.

Cohen, D. (1993) *How to Succeed in Psychometric Tests*, Sheldon Press.

Cohen, L. (1994) Brands and Valuations. *Managing Intellectual Property*, June.

Cook, T. (1995) Measuring the Benefits of Patent Protection. *Managing Intellectual Property*, June.

Copeland, T., Koller, T. and Murrin, J. (1995) *Valuation Measuring and Managing the Value of Companies*, John Wiley & Sons.

Crainer, S. (1995) *The Real Power of Brands*, Pitman.

Dar, V. K. (1995) The Future of the U.S Electric Utility Industry. *The Electricity Journal*, July.

Davidson, M. W. (1995) The Gene Kings. *Business Week*, May 22.

Davis, E. and Bannock, G. (1991) *The Nestlé Takeover Of Rowntree*, The David Hume Institute.

Davis, E. and Kay, J. (1990) Assessing Corporate Performance. *Business Strategy Review*, Summer.

Davis, R. and Lenat, D. B. (1982) *Knowledge-Based Systems in Artificial Intelligence*, McGraw Hill Inc.

De Bono, E. (1985) *Six Thinking Hats*, Penguin Group.

De Marco, T. (1979) *Structured Analysis and System Specification*, Yourdon.

Deal, T. E. and Kennedy, A. A. (1982) *Corporate Cultures*, Addison Wesley.

Department of Trade and Industry (1991) *Total Quality Management and Effective Leadership*, October.

Donaldson, G. (1995) Strategic Audit. *Harvard Business Review*, July–Aug.

Donaldson, T. H. (1992) *The Treatment of Intangibles*, The Macmillan Press Ltd.

Drexler, K. E. (1990) *Engines of Creation*, Fourth Estate.

Dumaine, B. (1994) *Entrepreneurs*, Fortune, March 21.

Eisenstadt, M. (1978) *Artificial Intelligence Project*, The Open University.

Elliot, Sir G. (1990) *Mergers and Takeovers – Short- and Long-Term Issues*, The David Hume Institute.

Fahrenkrog, Dr G. and Boekholt, P. (1993) Workshop for 'Tacit Knowledge' Transfer, Commission Of The European Communities, May 19.

Fields, D. (1995) Scott Rolls Out – A Risky Strategy. *Business Week*, May 22.

Firlej, M. and Hellens, D. (1991) *Knowledge Elicitation*, Prentice Hall.

Flynn, J. and Melcher, R. (1993) Can Heineken Stay on the top Shelf? *Business Week*, August 1.

Flynn, J. and Zinn, L. (1993) Absolute Pandemonium. *Business Week*, November 22.

Fransman, M. (1994) *Information, Knowledge, Vision and Theories of the Firm*, Oxford University Press.

Garnsey, E. and Wilkinson, M. (1994) *Global Alliance in High Technology*, Pergamon.

Glazier, S. (1995) Inventing around your Competitors Patents. *Managing Intellectual Property*, July/August.

Goddard, J. and Houlder, D. (1995) Beyond Magic. *Business Strategy Review*, Spring.

Gowland, D. H. (1990) *Finance and Takeovers*, The David Hume Institute.

Gregoire, P. and Lamber, K. (1994) An Inside Look at Calpers Boardroom Report Card. *Business Week*, October 17.

Gropp, G. (1994) The Spawning of a Third Sector. *Business Week*, November 7.

Gumsey, H. L. (1989) *Some Historical Perspectives, Copyright, Competition and Industrial Design*.

Guptara, P. (1995) Networking on a Global Scale. *Business Alliances*, December 12.

Hall, P. and Dixon, R. (1988) *Franchising*, Pitman.

Hammer, M. and Champy, J. (1993) *Reengineering the Corporation*, Harper Collins.

Hammonds, K. (1993) Can Drugs 'R' Us Be Far Behind? *Business Week*, November 22.

Hanson, P. (1995) Benchmarking best practice in European manuafacturing sites. *Business Process Re-Engineering & Management Journal*, January.

Harvey, M. and Lusch, R. (1995) *Expanding The Nature And Scope Of Due Diligence*, Elsevier.

Helgesen, S. (1995) Webs of Inclusion. *Executive Excellence*, April 10.

Henderson, R. (1994) The Key to innovation is good management. *Harward Business Review*, Jan–Feb.

Hillier, J. and Littlefield, D. (1995) Questioning the value of NVQS. *People Management*, February 9.

Hofacker, R. (1992) Russian Invention Machine Wins Over Skeptics. *BellLabs News*, August 2.

Hoffmann, E. (1994) Finally the Jinx may be off Jaguar. *Business Week*, October 10.

Hower, R. (1995) Quadrant, Guardian of the Famous and the Dead. *Business Week*, May 8.

Huey, J. (1994) Waking Up to the New Economy. *Fortune*, June 27.

Humphris, C. (1994) The Complete Guide to Computer Law. *Business Technology Magazine*.

Imai, M. (1986) *Kaizen*, McGraw-Hill.

Investors in People UK (1994) *An Introduction to Investors in People*, Department of Trade and Industry.

Investors in People UK (1995) *How to get Started*, Department of Trade and Industry.

Investors in People UK (1995) *The Benefits of being an Investor in People*, Department of Trade and Industry.

Investors in People UK (1995) *What's in it for me?* Department of Trade and Industry.

Jackson, J. O. (1995) Off the Screen. *Time*, July.

Kaplan, R. and Norton, D. (1993) Putting the Balanced Scorecard to Work. *Harvard Business Review*, Sept–Oct.

Kazarian, P. (1995) Raider on the Net. *Business Week*, October 23.

Keirsey, D. and Bates, M. (1978) *Please Understand Me: Character & Temperament Types*, Prometheus Nemesis.

Kelley, R. (1988) In Praise of Followers. *Harvard Business Review*, Nov–Dec.

Kennedy, S. (1993) *Goodwill and Intangible Assets*, The Accounting Standards Board.

Klinker, G. (1993) *The Active Glossary*, Academic Press Limited.

Laing, D. (1993) *Music and Copyright – Copyright and The International Music Industry*, Edinburgh University Press.

Lansner, E. (1993) The Eurosion Of Brand Loyalty. *Business Week*, July 19.

Lead Body Member Organisations (1994) *Vocational Standards and Qualifications In Marketing*, The Marketing Standards Board Lead Body, November.

Lehman, B. and Wild, J. (1994) Lehman's Law. *Mananging Intellectual Property*, December.

Lloyd, I. J. (1993) *Information Technology Law*, Butterworth & Co.

Main, B. and Johnston, J. (1992) *The Remuneration Committee as an Instrument of Coporate Governance*, The David Hume Institute.

Marchand, D. (1996) The Information Infrastructure. *Mastering Management*, January 9.

McCorduck, P. (1979) *Machines Who Think*, W. H. Freeman and Company.

Martin, J. and Odell, J. (1995) *Object Oriented Methods*, Prentice Hall.

Martin, S. (1995) A Futures Market for Competencies. *People Management*, March 23.

Mattimore, B. (1993) The Amazing Machine. *Success*, October.

Mendelsohn, M. (1985) *The Guide to Franchising*, Pergamon Press.

Mendelsohn, M. (1989) *Franchise Your Business*, 3rd edn, Stoy Hayward Franchising Services.

Mendelsohn, M. (1989) *Franchise Internationally*, Franchise World Magazine.

Menzel, P. (1994) Rethinking Work. *Business Week*, October 17.

Mitchell, G. (1993) Patent Showdown Pending. *Business Week*, May 10.

Morgan, E. V. and Morgan, A. D. (1990) *Investment Managers and Takeovers-Information Attitudes*, The David Hume Institute.

Morgan, E. V. and Morgan, A. D. (1990) *The Stock Market and Mergers in the United Kingdom*, The David Hume Institute.

Morita, A. (1987) *Made in Japan*, Fontana.

Morris, P. (1995) Will so many ingredients work together? *Business Week*, March 27.

Munchau, W. (1995) Lingering death of AEG – a lesson in mismanagment. *Financial Times*, December 20.

Murphy, J. (1989) *Brand Valuation*, 2nd edn, Business Books.

Negroponte, N. (1995) *Being Digital*, Hodder & Stoughton.

O'Brien, R. Cruise (1995) Is Trust a Calculable Asset in the Firm? *Business Strategy Review*, Winter.

Ostrom, E. (1995) *Self-organization and Social Capital*, Oxford University Press.

Otfinowski, D. (1995) We Won't Stop Until We Find Our Way Back. *Business Week*, May 1.

Parr, R. L. (1991) *Investing in Intangible Assets*, John Wiley & Sons.

Pemberton, Dr J. M. and McBeth, Dr R. (1995) Opportunities Out Of Chaos. *Records Management Quarterly*, July.

Pheysey, D. C. (1993) *Organizational Cultures*, Routledge.

Porter, M. (1987) Corporate Strategy. *The Economist*, May 23.

PR Week, survey.

Prince, R. (1994) Reinventing Xerox. *Black Enterprise*, June.

Psychological Corporation (1996) Occupational Assessement Catalogue.

Quintas, P. and Guy, K. (1993) Collaborative Pre-Competitive R&D and the Firms. *Research Policy*, November.

Quittner, J. (1995) Wiring the World. *Time*, July.

Raab, S. and Matusky, G. (1987) *The Blueprint For Franchising A Business*, John Wiley & Son.

Rabino, S. and Enayati, E. (1995) *Intellectual Property: The Double Edged Sword*, Pergamon, October.

Rawnsley, J. (1995) *Going For Broke*, Harper Collins.

Reid, G. (1990) *Efficient Markets And The Rationale Of Takeovers*, The David Hume Institute.

Richter, F.-J. and Vettel, K. (1995) *Successful Joint Ventures in Japan*, Pergamon.

Ries, A. and Trout, J. (1981) *Positioning The Battle For Your Mind*, McGraw-Hill.

Roberts, K. (1995) The Proof of HR is in the Profits. *People Management*, February 9.

Roddick, A. (1992) *Body And Soul*, Vermilion.

Rohrabacher, D. and Crilly, P. (1995) The Case For A Strong Patent System. *Harvard Journal of Law & Technology*, Spring.

Rosenthal, R. (1968) *McLuhan*, Penguin Books.

Rosenthal, Z. (1993) For Hollywood, These Are Truly The Dogs Days. *Business Week*, July 5.

Rowan, M. (1993) Cadbury's thrust parried by business. *Financial Director*, October 24.

Rust, J. and Golombok, S. (1989) *Modern Psychometrics*, Routledge.

Samuels, C. (1995) How Delata Flew Circles Around Pan Am In Court. *Business Week*, Feb 20.

Saville & Holdsworth Ltd (1996) Assessment Materials.

Saville & Holdsworth Ltd, Why People are Important.

Saville & Holdsworth Ltd (1995) Price List, 1 October.

Saville & Holdsworth Ltd (1996) Training Programmes.

Saville & Holdsworth Ltd, Occupational Psychology Tests.

Seibold, J O. (1993) The Global Patent Race Picks Up Speed. *Science & Technology*, August 9.

Skandia (1994) *Visualizing Intellectual Capital in Skandia*. Supplement to Annual Report.

Sinclair, D. and Zairi, M. Effective Process Management through Performance Measurment. *Business Process Re-Engineering & Management Journal*. Annual Report.

Smith, G. V. and Parr, R. L. (1989) *Valuation of Intellectual Property and Intangible Assets*, John Wiley & Sons.

Smythe, J. and Pickard, J. (1995) Harvesting the Office Grapevine. *People Management*, September 7.

Schneider, C. (1995) The Advertising Age. *The Sunday Times*.

Stanworth, J. and Smith, B. (1991) *Franchising*, Blackwell.

Stewart, D. (1986) *The Power of People Skills*, John Wiley & Sons.

Talley, D. J. (1991) *Total Quality Management*, ASQC Quality Press.

Thompson, P. and Wallace, T. (1992) The Urge to Merge. *The International Journal of Human Resource*, September.

Thornburg, L. (1995) HR in the Year 2010. *HR Magazine*, May.

Thronburg, L. (1994) Accounting for Knowledge. *HR Magazine*, October.

Tung, R. (1994) Human Resource Issues and Technology Transfer. *The International Journal of Human Resources Management*, December.

van der Spek, R. (1995) AI Watch, December.

Vella, R. (1994) Mom and Pop go High Tech. *Business Week*, November 21.

Veronsky, F. (1993) American News Crisis Management. *Businss Week*, July 5.

von Oech, R. (1986) *A Kick In The Seat Of The Pants*, Harper Perennial.

von Oech, R. (1983) *A Whack On The Side Of The Head*, Creative Think.

Waterman, R. H. and Waterman, J. A. (1994) Toward a Career Resilient Workforce. *Harvard Business Review*, July–Aug.

Weber, J., Flynn, J. and Lowry, K. (1994) Smithklines New World Order. *Business Week*, September 12.

Weyer, M. V. (1995) Ups and Down of the People Business. *Management Today*, June.

Wielinga, R. and Boose, J. (1990) *Current Trends In Knowledge Acquisition*, IOS.

Wiig, K. M. (1993) *Knowledge Management Foundation*, Schema Press.

Wild, J. (1994) Virgin on the real thing. *Mananging Intellectual Property*, November.

Winblad, A. L. and Edwards, S. D. (1990) *Object-Oriented Software*, Addison Wesley.

Winfrey, F. and Michalisin, M. (1995) *Super-Organizations*, John Wiley & Sons.

Winston, P. H. (1984) *Artificial Intelligence*, Addison Wesley.

Yoshimori, M. (1995) *Who's Company is it?* Pergamon.

Young, D. and Sutcliffe, B. (1990) *Value Gaps, Who Is Right – The Raiders, The Market or the Managers*, Pergamon Press.

Yourdon, E. and Constantine, L. L. (1979) *Structured Design*, Prentice Hall.

Zabriskie, N. and Huellmantel, A. (1994) *Marketing Research as a Strategic Tool*, Permagon.

INDEX

Page numbers in **bold** refer to figures; page numbers in *italics* refer to tables

About the Author

Annie Brooking, Managing Director and founder of The Technology Broker, has worked in the high technology industry for 24 years. She is recognized in the areas of tactical and strategic marketing, management, strategic planning, technology and the emerging area of intellectual capital. She has held management and executive positions at Sun Microsystems Inc. and at Symbolics Inc. in the USA, where she directed the marketing group and was responsible for the successful negotiation of multi-million dollar strategic alliances. She has had extensive international consulting experience with both start-up companies and billion dollar corporations on both management and technical issues.

Brooking founded and managed Europe's first industrial artificial intelligence research and consulting group, The Knowledge Based Systems Centre in the United Kingdom. She has served as a consultant to the European Economic Community in Brussels on advanced information processing for twelve years. In addition, in 1983 she designed the first successful advanced information processing project for the CEC's project ESPRIT, *A methodology for the design of knowledge based systems.*

Brooking has lectured widely both publicly and in academic institutions on numerous topics related to computer science and high technology. During her early career she worked as an academic, holding a variety of teaching posts at South Bank and Brunel Universities. She is co-author on two books on artificial intelligence and numerous papers on AI and Innovation topics.

Brooking's extensive expertise and contacts throughout the world give her insight into how industry can best use technologies for profit. She has completed post graduate studies in computer science at Brunel University in the UK.

Brooking has lived in the UK, Malta, Australia, and the US. She now lives with her husband Andrew on a small holding in Cambridge, UK.

Annie Brooking can be contacted at The Technology Broker on:
Phone: +44-(0)-1954-261199
FAX : +44-(0)-1954-260291
e-mail: annie@tbroker.co.uk
http://www.enterprise.net/tbroker

BRADNER LIBRARY
SCHOOLCRAFT COLLEGE
18600 HAGGERTY ROAD
LIVONIA, MICHIGAN 48152